RESURRECTING TRASH:

DAN PHILLIPS AND THE PHOENIX COMMOTION

Edited by

Doug Haines, Senior Editor

with Don R. Bates, Amanda Dellett, Christina Fernandez, Jake Gebhardt,
Anna R. Jennings, Dustin Levien, Lauren McAuliffe, and Margaret Miller Sellers

Texas Review Press
Huntsville, Texas

Printed in the United States of America

FIRST EDITION, 2013
Requests for permission to reproduce material from this work should be sent to:

Permissions
Texas Review Press
English Department
Sam Houston State University
Huntsville, TX 77341-2146

Acknowledgments:

The editors wish to thank Dan and Marsha Phillips and the Phoenix Commotion and all associated contributors to this volume. Without your assistance, the book would not have been possible.

Library of Congress Cataloging-in-Publication Data

Resurrecting trash : Dan Phillips and the Phoenix Commotion / Doug Haines ... [et al.].

p. cm.

ISBN 978-1-933896-86-1 (pbk. : alk. paper)

1. Ecological houses--Texas--Huntsville. 2. Phoenix Commotion (Organization) 3. Phillips, Dan, 1946- 4. House construction--Materials--Texas--Huntsville. 5. Waste products as building materials--Texas--Huntsville. 6. Building materials--Recycling--Texas--Huntsville. 7. Salvage (Waste, etc.)--Texas--Huntsville. 8. Construction industry--Texas--Huntsville. I. Haines, Doug, 1975-

TH4860.R47 2012

691--dc23

2012044070

This book is dedicated to

Dan and Marsha Phillips

and

the Phoenix Commotion

Table of Contents

Foreword

I have watched Dan Phillips at work for nearly forty years, and I must say that he constantly surprises me with his ability to create something magnificent out of "trash" others have consigned to the city dump or left at the curb to be hauled off by anyone who wants it. License plates, shattered tiles, bottle caps, wine corks, gnarled bois d'arc limbs, sawed-off ends of timber—in the hands of this master craftsman all become the finest and most versatile of building materials. He is a magician in the world of home construction. In this book you will learn all about Dan and The Phoenix Commotion and be introduced to some of his remarkable projects.

When my 2012 Editing/Publishing Practicum class met for the first time, I had Dan address the students; before the class was over, he had them mesmerized and totally sold on his philosophy of life and construction. There was no question in their minds but that they wanted to do a book on Dan Phillips and The Phoenix Commotion.

This is a class in which students learn how to make a book from beginning to end: They do the initial research, organize the materials, outline the book, write the text, lay out photos and illustrations, and design the cover, all with as little input from me as possible. I was there to advise and help out when problems arose, but the book is their baby, from conception to delivery, complete with whatever blemishes you might detect.

Resurrecting Trash: Dan Phillips and the Phoenix Commotion was a particularly difficult book, unlike any the class has ever done before. The students devoted hundreds of hours of research to it, involving long interviews with Dan and those associated with his many projects; making dozens of trips to many of the houses, parks, and businesses involved; taking hundreds of photos; and sorting through hundreds of photographs from outside sources. Past classes have produced books on the Wynn Home in Huntsville, Texas High School Mascots, Hurricane Katrina, and creative writing and art by Texas Death Row inmates, and all have involved photographs and illustrations, but no project ever came close to the complexity this class experienced as they wrote and laid out this book. Given the range of dimensions of the photos, there was no way that the student editors could design and employ a template, so each one had to be placed individually and sized according to available space. The quality of the photographs, many of them quite old and/or of poor initial quality, was an issue quite beyond their ability to address in some instances: They did the best they could with what they managed to get their hands on.

I would like especially to thank Doug Haines, who devoted four full months of his time during the summer and fall of 2012, without pay, to rewriting and restructuring much of the book. Without his devotion to the project, the book would not be released until late in 2013. I would further like to thank Ruth Irvin, one of my Texas Review Press interns, for her many hours of rewriting and copyediting.

Most of all, I would like to thank Dan and Marsha Phillips for graciously consenting to allow my class to develop a book that should have been released by a commercial publisher years ago.

Paul Ruffin, Director, Texas Review Press

RESURRECTING TRASH:

DAN PHILLIPS AND THE PHOENIX COMMOTION

Dan Phillips: Trash in His DNA

by Margaret Miller Sellers

"What is the point of having a nice house, if you don't have a decent planet to put it on?" ~Henry David Thoreau

[We] are smart about our arrogance and humble about the opportunities the planet has provided: the melding of unbelievable technology at our fingertips with "homespun" and on-site strategies, a new toolbox, as it were, to leave the smallest footprint possible with no loss of quality of life. There are primitive pleasures in "chopping our own wood" and "hauling our own water," pleasures we haven't been privy to for a century. We can re-sensitize synapses that have long ago atrophied. There's still time. And I want to be a part of that. ~Dan Phillips

Dan Phillips, founder of the Phoenix Commotion, a building initiative in Huntsville, Texas, wants to prove that the construction of homes using recycled and salvaged materials holds a worthwhile place in the building industry. He met with me to interview in September of 2011, and he candidly shared things about every aspect of his life—from childhood to the development of his philosophy.

Dan does not exactly fit into the structured sense of what it is to be successful when you first meet him. He has a sort of unkempt long gray ponytail and isn't concerned about the latest fashion. When we met, Dan wore jean-shorts, a T-shirt, and work boots—continually drinking coffee served from a beat-up thermos (purchased for him by his wife years ago at a garage sale). According to his workers and volunteers, he never eats, and his thin, gaunt frame seems to confirm it. While Dan is not rich in the material sense, he is extremely wealthy in a different way. He told me repeatedly throughout the day that he loves his life.

Our interview was conducted just past the Hitch'in Post Truck Stop at the Burdett Recycling Center near exit 118 in Huntsville. When driving to our designated meeting place, I saw a Home Depot. Having done my homework on Dan, I didn't have to wonder if he would ever set foot in a commercialized building store like that—I knew better. The magazine and newspaper articles about Dan and the Phoenix Commotion made very clear that his choice of suppliers for building projects is a choice of conscience, and the usual picks are the recycling center or landfill.

He calls what he finds there "candy," claiming that the dumps hold all the "human detritus," or materials that have been rejected because they were not perfect.

The articles I read also explained that Dan's recycling and

Handmade Houses, ***by Art Boericke and Barry Shapiro. This book influenced Dan to work with recycled products.***

salvaging philosophy has created for him a strong presence in the United States, a following across Europe, and a long list of volunteers from all backgrounds and locations. I wondered how a house built from recycled materials was so different from the perfect little beige houses lined up side-by-side in my neighborhood, or how anyone could teach himself how to build a house out of those materials from the ground up. More baffling still is the idea that Dan completely disregarded the standard building industry business formula in favor of this more economical alternative, a risky, though not new, trend in the market.

Dan says he is part of a larger army of people who have been building with recycled materials for many years. He says, "Today, what is available is trash, so that is what we are using." Some of his influences include Mike Reynolds, the founder of Earthship Biotecture, and Samuel Sambo Mockbee, the architecture professor at Auburn University who founded the Auburn Rural Studio Program. His influences are not limited to these business leaders, though. Some of Dan's other influences are the books *Being and Nothingness*, by Jean-Paul Sartre, and *Handmade Houses: A Guide to the Woodbutcher's Art*, written by Art Boericke and Barry Shapiro. The latter book, filled with pictures of the most unusual and beautiful structures built out of recycled materials, introduced him to building with material from landfills and junkyards. Dan's philosophy—and vision in life and business—of living free and building without restriction is paralleled in the introduction:

For some years we have heard the extravagant technological promise of housing at a low cost. It has never come to pass. The answer to low-cost housing, it seems to me, is to make a break with a "standard of living" that makes us slaves to centralized decision-making and control, to an economy whose values are the magnitude of production and consumption. The dollar is not a reasonable measure of the quality of life or the quality of place.

The discussion of this book sparked a broader conversation about how the attitudes of Americans have been skewed by the marketplace and are reflected in the cars we drive, the clothes we wear, and the houses we build. He explained: "We are a social species and we are trying to belong. We are all victims of this. I am sensitive that it needs to make sense, that there is a social contract."

The fear Americans have of using recycled materials, or materials that appear to be imperfect, Dan blames on the human struggle of dealing with social pressures:

There are expectations in society down to the houses we build. We are a social species. We are trying to belong to a group. We will do what they are doing over there. It is tough for people to be mediocre. It is tough for people to fail. If you don't have the nerve, you are liv-

ing the other way. The safe way. It would be nice if we could use our own ideas to manifest [the expectations].

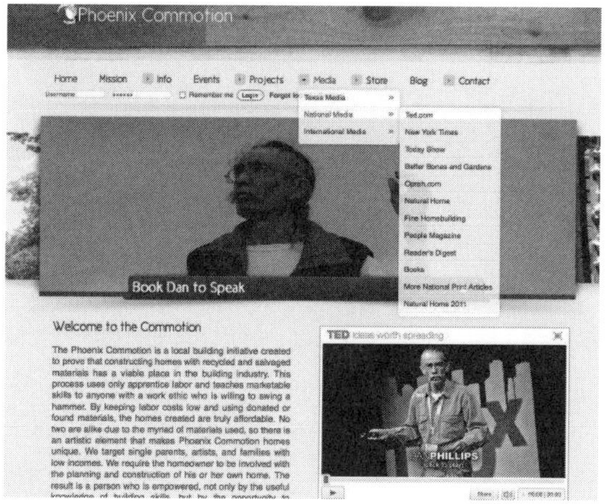

These social pressures to conform have caused people to lose the nerve to nurture an idea on their own.

So came the question: Does Dan live with recycled materials on the walls and papier-mâché flooring? His answer shows just how little he tolerates waste:

We have papier-mâché and tile-shard floors, but we also have wall-to-wall carpet in our house. It is like walking on dirty socks. Can't clean it with a broom. I have a dishwasher. I never use it anymore. These things won't get replaced. We are all victims of a cultural mindset that has been developing for over 200 years. You have to be gentle about that. Any charge I would level onto someone else, I would level on myself.

This led me to wonder why he chose this path. "Why do you do this for a living?" I asked Dan, unsure of exactly how anyone makes a drastic career choice like starting the Phoenix

Crew on roof of T.J. Burdett & Sons office building

Recycled gazebo

Commotion. He responded simply that he does it because he can. Dan's requirements for happiness are limited. His most frivolous desire is to have an occasional prime-rib steak with a side of horseradish and a good cabernet sauvignon. He's immersed in a struggle to hold onto the purity of design and a philosophy that is important to him, while simultaneously resisting the pressure of bending toward the dollar. Somehow, every day he resists giving in to building budgets and bank demands out of the need to survive.

Dan sees beauty in everything. Rejected pieces of granite become incredible walls, and used bottle caps transform into mosaic floors. But more than the beauty of material things, Dan sees intrinsic beauty in the people he works with on the job sites.

Bottle cap chair by Edie Wells

He also enjoys helping people: "Giving back and helping people yields a life that is absolutely unmatched. When you help people, they will do anything for you. We are all like this. I just have the opportunity. My life is the perfect storm." So he helps by empowering people daily to rise above their problems and let go of the rules that limit the imagination. At times, this empow-

The crew at the Waste Management Grand Opening August 8th, 2011

erment is a gesture as simple as leaving them with a pile of material and telling them to work with it. At this point, they have a "blank slate." It is up to them to create what they will. According to Dan, he is not an artist—he is a designer. The way he talks about creative freedom seems to imply otherwise. He had something to say about the artist's blank slate:

Most people are paralyzed by a blank slate. The difference in building design comes with the way someone responds to this blankness. I take a pile of stuff and say, this is kinda fun. Let's try this! After a while, your work takes on a life of its own. The artwork evolves as you go through it. You allow what you create to speak to you. Suddenly the dynamics of what you have done shoot over you. Same way with building with trash or writing music. Talk to any composer or painter. Where do you start? You start with something and it piques your imagination. If you press through, the payoff is fantastic. It teaches you so much.

Recycled bathroom

It is no surprise that Dan empowers people, seeing that he takes the time to get to know them. He can tell you everything about his employees and volunteers. He knows the good stuff, and the bad stuff, and he takes them exactly as they are. He never loses sight of the importance of the people. He tries to inspire this in the people around him, too. For example, if he knows someone working with him is having a hard time, he's been known to ask some of his other workers to add kind words of support or encouragement throughout the day. The product is a work environment like no other. All day the worksites comprise a group of people that are always smiling and that work tirelessly together as a team.

Dan helps artist Sabrina Bedford

Picture-frame sample ceiling in artist studio

I observed some of his workers cutting pieces of old signs to hang on the walls of the upcoming Burdett Recycling Center office. Others were helping remodel the upstairs office space. They chatted with each other, took breaks together, and laughed about Dan when they were asked about him. They said he was a great boss. And even when I prodded them, explaining that they didn't have to hold back the bad stuff, no one had anything negative to say.

Dan and his wife of 42 years, Marsha.

Dan's employees get the concept behind The Phoenix Commotion projects, which is a huge part of the reason he takes non-professional, inexperienced workers. He wants his philosophy to carry through these people like a legacy. He accepts his role as a front man for this cause, so he spends time traveling and lecturing—and he is pretty comfortable attending to those aspects of his mission. One of his favorite narratives involves making ornamental features for housing from egg shells: "You have to eat breakfast first, and then fill the shells with bondo and paint them." He tends to get a good laugh from the crowd with that one.

Papier-mâché floor by Edie Wells

Beer-label papier-mâché floor by Linda Zapalac

The Phoenix Commotion workers speak of Dan enthusiastically. One man, George Boone, works with Dan and is building his own house out of recycled materials. He called Dan creative and went as far as to label him "a Found-Object Artist much like Picasso." George said that "Dan wants to see things practically. He wants to use recycled materials in a real way. If not, he would do whatever everyone else is doing, which is 'cookie cutter.' I think there are negatives with being called an artist. That's why."

Dan speaks to whoever will listen.

Other employees talked about the philosophy Dan expounds upon, like pieces of Gesalt Psychology, Nietzsche, and references to John Dewey's *Art As Experience*. When he discusses these theories, he clearly displays high emotion, increased voice intonation, and rapid eye movement.

Another volunteer, Alex Cunningham, 22, sent Dan an email last summer asking him if he could fly over from Oxford, England, to work with him. Many weeks later, Dan told him to come to Texas if he could pay his own way. Alex's field of study is Engineering, and he believes, just as Dan does, that working with recycled products is very important. He wants to be a responsible builder, and sharing from his experience he said: "Dan makes you want to change things."

Dan and Marsha's wedding '69

This response from Alex is why Dan has challenged the construction business to think about the value of the many products left behind in landfills. He sees potential in everything and everyone. When I asked him what the traditional builders in the area say about his work, he responded "Well, they build the way they do and I build the way I do. I don't have to do what they do." And this is his classic response. Knowing a little bit about Dan's life helps to reveal why.

Dan has been married to his wife, Marsha, for 42 years, with two successful children to show for it. Their son, Ian, is an F-16 pilot and a Lt. Colonel. He and his wife Karen, a general surgeon, have two children, Luke and Mason. Their daughter, Phoebe, and her husband Al are both attorneys who also have two children, Shephard and Reese. When Dan told me that he sees his kids a few times a year, I asked him if they knew about the attention he is receiving. He modestly replied, "They know."

Kitchen counter made from broken tile and mirror shards

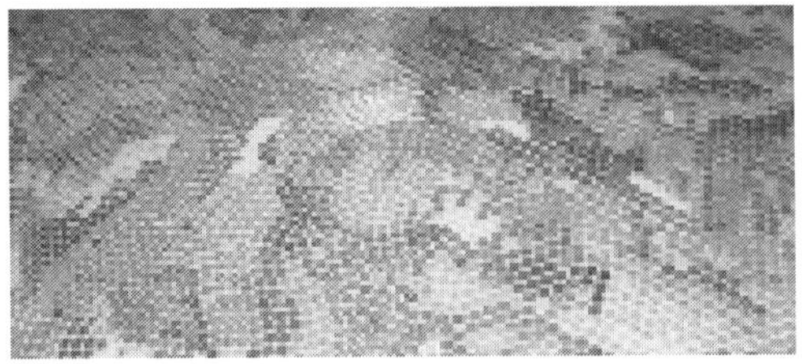

Bottle cap floor done by the crew

When Dan was thinking of starting the Phoenix Commotion, he knew his plan violated a sense of logic, but he still offered Marsha this different type of business proposal:

I said, Marsha, what do ya think? Marsha, what I would like to do is mortgage our house and wipe out our savings. We will build for people who have abdicated all responsibility and have no credit. We will build them out of trash. What do ya think? [He laughs a little.] *I'm still married.*

When I asked Dan about her reaction, he said that she thought it would be fun. Marsha is a former high school art teacher and an integral player in the Phillips' business. They now live off her part-time job, perhaps with Social Secuirty benefits kicking in before long. He doesn't feel bad about it; in fact, he appears to be without worry. But he didn't get to this place of solace without some struggle and a learned gritty sense of determination.

Stained-glass window by Linda Zapalac

Born in 1945, Dan was the youngest of three children

Neko Richardson at work

in the secure, middle-class home of George and Phoebe. George owned a lumber company and Phoebe was a homemaker. His father had a bit of bad luck in business, which resulted in the family moving to Littleton, Colorado.

Dan's sister, Alice, married while he was still very young. He boasts that she was once given the Ms. Colorado World title: "Oh, yes, she was a dish." Alice and her husband at one time owned a landfill in Colorado before moving to Las Vegas, where she was the executive secretary for many casinos over the years:

That was an interesting time for her. She set up complimentary perks to attract gamblers. She would arrange all these amenities for them. In return, they gave her lots of fancy gifts. Her closets were filled with thousands of dollars worth of perfume.

Eyebrow dormer on Storybook House

While he was reminiscing about Alice, I asked Dan what type of relationship they have. Much like many other adult siblings, he said they haven't been in each other's lives much but were always there for each other.

His other sibling, John, eight years Dan's senior, was his hero. He spent a lot of time trying to impress him. Like any younger brother, he imitated the things John did—even if that imitation was something as terrifying as Brahma bull riding. He said that his brother expected him to ride. Dan, 12 at the time, and small-framed at less than 100 pounds, did just that. "It was all just a blur until I found myself in the dirt. It taught me a lot. You face things head-on. You are petrified, but you do it anyway."

Front view of T.J. Burdett & Sons office building

Part of the decision for the family to move to Littleton had to do with his brother falling into the wrong crowd as a teenager, which Dan discusses openly. John continued to have some problems with alcohol over the years, but was very bright. He designed a fun house for a traveling carnival, and Dan helped him. It was obvious that this experience with John and the

Road-sign ceiling

carnival had an impact on him: "Carnies are a tough, tight-knit group, and everybody involved has to learn how to work the money. The carnival taught me how to spit and scratch and how to negotiate with people in general." The carnival taught him to deal with the tougher side of people. In fact, he is constructing the Burdett Recycling office building as part of a trade deal that he put together. Burdett gets an office building at a lower cost, and Dan gets land space to store products and supplies on the grounds of the recycling center. Having graduated from high school in Golden in 1963, Dan was in college at the Univesity of Northern Colorado at this point, and he spent his summers working the carnival circuit.

His brother continued to get into trouble over the years, eventually going into the service. Dan mentioned again that John was very smart and talented, softly explaining that his brother aced the test to become an engineer at Continental. Unfortunately, he got drunk and didn't make it to the interview. Dan said, "He missed out on all that." Sadly, John later died from chronic alcoholism.

Burdett's logo, "Uncle Sam wants your can!" created by crew member Matt Gifford

Seriously and quietly, Dan explained that he didn't know his father well because he disappeared when Dan was seventeen. He told me that he had visited a psychic several years ago, finally burying the idea that he would ever see his father again. As a teen, with his father mostly out of the picture, his mother became the strong influence.: "My mother did all the cabinet work. She was an artist herself. We always had ceramics around. She did jewelry and carvings." He related to this about his mother. Dan always wanted to build things: "I think it's in everyone's DNA to want to be a builder," he said, commenting that he built his own bike out of materials from a landfill at age 14. "Once you realize you can create stuff, it bleeds into every corner of your life."

Dan, Eagle Scout

But Dan's education was not in engineering or building; rather, he earned a BA in English from what is now Northern Colorado University, an MA from Sam Houston State University in 1969, and an Ed.D in 1974 from the University of North Carolina at Greensboro. He did research for his dissertation at the libraries in West Berlin while serving in the military in intellegence analysis. Before gettting into building, Dan was a dance instructor at Sam Houston State University for nine years. He believes that he uses his experience with dance in all parts of his construction business:

Alice & Dan

The fluid motions of art have to obey the same rules as the motions of the body. The thing about it is that the body tells you so much. When you are a dancer, you have to focus on your body. You have to know how to relax your shoulders. Everything has to be automatic and relaxed. You learn to know your body so well. If you listen to the body, you feel it if something is a little disproportioned. It's not quite right. That is prelanguage. That

Dan's grandmother, great grandmother, his parents, and his bother, John

is how we make our decisions every day. All the principal elements of art—balance, rhythm, contrast, and unity—are how we actually think. Those are basic human cravings in design. Our sense of gravity informs our sense of design. I lived the better part of my life as a dancer. I listen to my body.

Dan the Explorer

Dan's ability to use dance as a filter truly sets his projects apart from the *Sanford and Son* look of just merely putting trash together.

Dan is a self-taught carpenter, electrician, and plumber, but has held a variety of different positions, including working as an intelligence analyst, an antiques dealer, and a syndicated cryptogram puzzle maker.

He applied for a teaching-assistant position at the University of North Carolina in the 1960s as part of his plan to avoid the draft, but the position ended and he made the decision to enlist. "There was the famous box that you could check. I indicated that I wanted language school because my experience with dance was closely associated with the French and Italian cultures," he told me. Very soon after enlisting, he was asked to assist with intelligence in West Berlin. His MOS (military occupational specialty) in the Army was 98G3LGM. As a German linguist, he was responsible for translating German intelligence into English at Field Station Berlin in West Berlin. Dan shared with me some interesting experiences in West Berlin:

When I first arrived at Andrews Barracks in Lichterfelde (a section of West Berlin), the compound was the former Cadet School for the Weimer Republic. They had an Olympic-sized swimming pool, where the 1938 Olympics were held, and huge dormitories with 16-foot ceilings. Hitler had installed a maze of tunnels connecting the various buildings outside the compound. When the Allies arrived at the compound at the end of WWII, the pool was filled to the brim with corpses, as were the tunnels. They simply sealed off the tunnels with huge steel plates, leaving the hu-

A proud Dan with his Brahma Bull riding trophy at age 16

man remains. That gave the compound an eerie feel, and stories flew about ghosts that would make themselves evident from time to time.

When I asked him if he enjoyed the experience, he replied:

Dan on trail crew for the Forestry Service

It taught me a lot about people. I realized it was all pretty much a game. I was participating in a larger scheme of manipulating people. I was being kind of exploited. I was also bored. West Berlin had a wall around it in those days. I was stuck there because of my security clearance. That was hard. The government couldn't take the risk of someone capturing me.

An early set of bois d'arc stairs

Upon returning to the states, Dan was approached by a mysterious person asking him if he wanted a job in intelligence: "They damn sure knew who I was," he said.

Back home, Dan started raising money for a small newspaper syndicate that he promoted to numerous newspapers and magazines around the country. He had developed a logic puzzle based on intersecting sets, titled "Brain Squeeze." Dan explained that the puzzle business is a "crowded room" and that "If you do get your foot in the door,

The young family

you are there until you die because there are loud readership complaints when a popular puzzle is replaced. Puzzles are addictive. That business is very difficult." The syndicate held together for twenty-five years.

Dan and Marsha made their move to their current home in Huntsville around 1974 and he began to work with antiques: "We had nothing. We slept on the floor until we could afford exactly the bed we wanted. This is when I first learned to glue and repair antiques." They operated an antique restoration business, The Phoenix Workshop, before the birth of the Phoenix Commotion. Dan said of this business that "he was rescuing art."

Dan had a lot to say about this part of his and Marsha's life:

Balance, rhythm, and contrast . . .

Tile fragments put to use, by Kristie Stevens

After nine years at Sam Houston State University, my wife and I were very interested in antiques. I didn't know much about it until we married. I started to cultivate this interest. Marsha grew up around antiques. Her family had antiques from all over the world.

Dan, wife Marsha, daughter Phoebe, and son Ian

Dan (top row, middle) with his dance students

By the time I resigned from the university, we had an opportunity to buy an antiques-refinishing business. Marsha and I and Jim Miller, who was of the head of the Drama Department, bought the business together. Later we bought him out. That was about 1982. When people asked me if I knew how to do something with refinishing an antique, I would say, sure, I will do it. If you like it, I will charge you. If you don't, I won't. I taught myself to repair almost anything and learned the process of gluing and refinishing, color matching, and retouching oil paintings. This experience taught me a lot. I was simply rescuing things from the deepest of holes.

Kitchen cabinets at the Oak Street Remodel

Marsha, Alice, and Dan

Dan explained that this is when and where his love affair with bone started:

There was ivory repair. The difference between ivory and bone is very small. I learned that bone is a great material. It is a great substitute. It had been completely overlooked. I had to repair mother-of-pearl on pool tables and such. I had a friend that had a big piece of something that looked like mother-of-pearl. He told me that it was not mother-of-pearl. My friend had been on a fishing dock. He had bought a squid that he took home, dried out, and then he put Hard as Nails polish on it. I tried this. I went and bought squid at an exotic fish market in Bellaire, Texas. However, I never got it to the point of drying it out because the crew I worked with complained about the smell. I built up a good reputation with this business, but it is hard to make a living restoring antiques.

Old Burdett signs form part of wall covering in Burdett office building

While Dan had the antique business, he was involved in a horrific fire that left him physically scarred. He still tears up when he thinks about it, and it was obviously difficult for him to talk about it. He explained that it had taught him a lot about himself:

It was 1995. We stripped furniture with an alcohol soup that was very dangerous and flammable. In an effort to keep my crew and myself safe from the fumes, I had built a contraption including a large steel syrup tank. I put the furniture on a table and closed the door to the tank. Nobody breathed the fumes. It seemed perfect. I soon learned you have to precipitate the fumes before you open this type of unit. This didn't happen. A cloud came out and caught a spark. I was burned over thirty-five percent of my body. I almost lost my ear and a piece of my nose. One of my employees was also burned. We both made it.

With a burn, a nutrient protein forms and has to be removed. They cleaned it off with the softest of gauze. It felt like they were cleaning it with a wire brush. There is a spot in the brain where you can turn off the pain, but it's hard to do.

Those people in those burn centers were excellent. I have the greatest respect for them. I will never complain again! It taught me a lot. Marsha was there throughout the whole experience. She didn't deserve that!

Dan always makes light of any situation that tends to get too serious. He finished the discussion about the fire by telling me that it was "a cauterizing experience."

Finally, in 1997 Dan and Marsha started The Phoenix Commotion. For a time, the businesses overlapped, but the workload was overwhelming, so the antique refinishing business closed its doors. They still own an antique store in Huntsville, though, so Dan still has "first dibs" on unusual pieces that come his way.

The Phoenix Commotion started with the purchase of two lots, on which Dan built houses primarily out of recycled materials. He usually builds in response to the need for affordable housing, but many of the homes are resold at a much higher value. The real value, though, is in the lasting mark left on the local community by Dan's creativity and vision, which reverberates across the country. He has been featured in *Houston House and Home, The New York Times, Natural Home & Garden,* and on numerous public television shows. Other recognitions Dan has received are: Most Innovative Housing Model Worldwide from the Institute for Social Invention in 2003, the Houston Hero Award in 2006, the Edison Green Award through Rutgers University in 2010, the Interfaith-Beacon Light Award in 2010, the Environmental Excellence Award given by TCEQ (Texas Commission on Environmental Quality) in 2010.

Spreading the reusable-materials gospel in Huntsville, Texas, accounts for a large part of Dan's community impact, but not all of it. He doesn't keep his model for building to himself, nor his opinions. Because of that, he participated in passing a building-inspection addendum in Houston, where there is a desperate need for affordable housing. The addendum is called Appendix R, which promotes Dan's belief that the perfect answer to a serious problem in the market is the use of recycled materials.

Developed by architect Amanda Tullos and Houston Building Code Administrator Sheila Blake, Appendix R is a set of guidelines designed to guide inspectors in reviewing recycled materials. Many of the inspectors would not even consider inspecting re-

Bone Tree at the Bone House

Marsha, Alice, and the kids

cycled materials before such an addendum. It took five years for Appendix R to pass, and Dan claims it will probably take ten to twenty years to get the building industry to pay attention to it. He said, "It is a start. They worked very hard and finally prevailed."

But outside of his work or public activism, Dan has made trash fashionable in the most authentic sense of "going green." Some people may think of the Green Movement as a fad or creative marketing device, but Dan is not driven by the dollar. He is not cornering the market with a competitive product or trying to develop a public relations campaign. He is the real thing. Dan Phillips truly desires to reduce the carbon footprint, and he has found a way to do that while also greatly impacting the people around him.

Proud Father of the Bride

A reason to think about the future

Spreading the gospel . . .

Dan making sketches

The Charleston House

Shannon Bryant works on a foundation

Former employee Josh Starkey's house

Bone Lawn Furniture at the Bone House

Highway signs in the Burdett office building

History of The Phoenix Commotion

History of The Phoenix Commotion

by Lauren McAuliffe & Dustin Levien

Not many people attempt to grapple with the vast and complex philosophical theories presented by such great thinkers as Nietzsche. They become overwhelmed with notions that take them outside the realms of thought they have always been comfortable with. The few who do proceed into such deep waters do so predominantly to enlighten themselves and gain a better understanding of the world around them.

This makes Dan Phillips exceptionally rare in that he has thoroughly garnered the insight of many great philosophers and put that insight into action by creating an organization founded on philosophy, but which benefits people who may never have heard of men like Nietzsche. Through The Phoenix Commotion, Dan is able to empower others with the insight he has gained. He takes theories, puts them into action, and then encourages others to do the same. The Phoenix Commotion is an organization whose purpose is to create original quality homes almost completely out of materials discarded by others. More specifically, the homes are built out of what most people perceive to be trash. As Dan puts it:

Dan just can't quit talking.

The Phoenix Commotion is a local building initiative created to prove that constructing homes with recycled and salvaged materials has a viable place in the building industry. This process uses only apprentice labor and teaches marketable skills to anyone with a work ethic who is willing to swing a hammer. By keeping labor costs low and using donated or found materials, the homes created are truly affordable. Due to the myriad of materials used, no two houses are alike, so there is an artistic element that makes Phoenix Commotion homes unique. We target single parents, artists, and families with low incomes. We require the homeowner to be involved with the planning and construction of his or her own home. The result is

Mosaic floor design/repetition

Cortina's House:

Martha and Joe Cortina, parents of five, built their own house using recycled materials with help from The Phoenix Commotion and local contractor/mentor Mike Bradley.

The Bone House: Artist's Studio

a person who is empowered, not only by the useful knowledge of building skills, but by the opportunity to become part of a community as a vested participant.

The Phoenix Commotion not only builds new homes from recycled materials—it builds up the people who live in those homes and allows them the opportunity to flourish. Dan's reasons for creating this organization are varied. He is not simply trying to solve one problem that he is passionate about. He is building the vision of a global community that is more aware of the consequences of its actions, and he encourages people to use their awareness and act on it to improve the quality of life for those who would not otherwise have a chance to do so. Concerned with people on both a vast and personal scale, he emphasizes that the luxuries of some will cause waste, which is to the detriment of everyone. His first goal in creating The Phoenix Commotion was to reduce the amount of waste that is discarded in landfills:

T.J. Burdett and Sons recycling operation

While an exact percentage is difficult to achieve, a reasonable estimate would be that 10% of the average landfill waste stream consists of usable building materials. Reclamation is practically impossible once these materials reach the landfill because of the immense liability involved. Municipal lawsuits tend to be large and last for years. In order to avoid possible lawsuits, most municipalities have simply forbidden salvage activity. There are, however, strategies for reclamation of materials before reaching such finality.

By encouraging people to see the possibility in materials

that are often discarded, Dan hopes to diminish the amount of refuse that already exists.

The next goal of The Phoenix Commotion is to provide quality housing for people who normally could not afford it. This will not only make it possible for people who are struggling to make ends meet to own their own home—it will also help them to feel that they are part of a community that respects and supports them. Dan explains this philosophy when he says,

Everyone must live somewhere. However, when a family owns its home, there is a conspicuous increase in overall self-esteem of its members and general family well-being, which ultimately leads to positive social results. The venues available to low-income families are rental property, public housing, or sheer luck. Purchase of a home is often out of reach for a low-income family because of the down-payment barrier. Further, low-income families typically have very little positive credit history. Many organizations, both public and private, are working hard in this area. The Phoenix Commotion is simply one more model in the private sector for solving such a complicated social problem.

For the reasons mentioned, Dan builds only for low-income families, single mothers, and artists. He also requires that any person who qualifies and wishes to have a home built by The Phoenix Commotion must be willing to share the responsibility by being involved in the home's construction from beginning to end. This way, the people who come to own the houses do so with a sense of pride because they are living in a house that they helped to build, and they possess the knowledge and skill to maintain it. Dan's dedication to helping others is not limited to the people he builds houses for. It extends to the people he hires to help him build those houses. He explains:

All workers on aftermarket houses are hired as unskilled laborers at minimum wage. Since one minimum-wage crew does all aspects of the construction, workers accumulate many marketable skills after a year on such a crew. They are then able to compete for higher-paying jobs. An unskilled crew does not mean "ineffective," however, as new skills can come quickly with proper tutelage.

Josh Starkey designed and is building his own home.

The people Dan hires help to prove that it is possible to build good-quality houses for very little by working for minimum wage. They learn not only the skills it takes to work for any construction company but also innovative ways to build outside of the constrictive norms that those companies have established.

Crew member Matt Gifford works on a mosaic.

Because of the dedication and innovation involved in this effort, Dan and The Phoenix Commotion have gained local, national, and global attention. Dan's work has been featured in *The New York Times*, *People Magazine*, *Fine Homebuilding*, *Reader's Digest*, and *Natural Home*. There is an article praising his contributions to society on Oprah.com, and he has also been featured on the *Today Show*. He has been the inspiration for several documentaries, and his organization has been the topic of news in Japan, Italy, Germany, Ireland, and China. The Phoenix Commotion is not just an organization built to better the Huntsville community. It simply took root there and has been spreading its influence to help improve communities all across the globe.

Shannon Bryant installs CDs on a ceiling.

By inspiring people to be creative and productive when constructing a house, Dan is able to prove his theory that it is possible to build houses out of recycled materials. Every home built under the supervision of The Phoenix Commotion is constructed of close to eighty percent found or discarded materials. Dan and his crew are constantly testing the boundaries of what they can use to build their homes. Where a less creative person would immediately throw old egg shells out (or, if they are more environmentally conscious, into a compost heap), Dan takes the shells, fills them with a resin, and uses them for architectural buttons. They fulfill the two requirements of materials that the crew hunts for: sturdy and readily available. Beyond those two requirements, a person searching for building materials is free to let his imagination run wild. Evidence of that freedom is seen running

Marissa Miller installs a papier-mâché floor.

Linda Zapalec grouts a mosaic.

rampant through each of Dan's houses. They are composed of materials that most people would not dream of using.

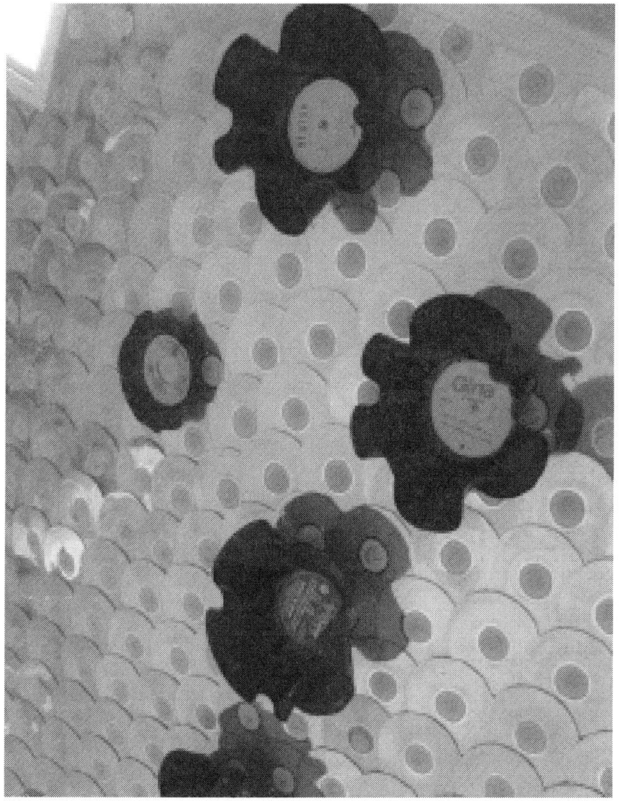

Edie Wells used CDs and vinyl records on a ceiling.

A good example of this is in the papier-mâché floors that have been used in several of the houses. The method for applying a papier-mâché floor is relatively simple and costs very little. It consists mainly of laying a single-ply paper down onto the floor and soaking it with thinned glue. It creates a strong floor covering that can be cleaned as easily as a more traditional one. This method also allows a person to make a floor that is an expression of his creativity and personality. The possibilities of design are endless because any type of paper can be used, from sheet music to comic-book pages. This means that every floor is as unique as the person building it.

Papier-mâché floors are not only a way for a home owner to express his creativity—they are also just as high in quality as more traditional floors, according to Dan:

Economy, durability, and design immediately present themselves as prime considerations in any floor covering. A papier-mâché floor accomplishes all of these things in about the same amount of time alternatives could be installed—sometimes more quickly. They can be as formal or as rustic as one chooses, can be damp-mopped, last for years, and are easily repairable.

George Boone installs a papier-mâché floor.

Dan's first concern is always with the quality of his materials. He is not trying to say that people who cannot afford "real houses" have to build theirs out of trash. He is striving to open people's minds to the fact that what they think of as "trash" is actually a resource with endless possibilities. A floor made out of sheet music or beer labels is only one example of a philosophy that The Phoenix Commotion is constantly putting into action.

Anyone who spends time near one of The Phoenix Commotion projects quickly finds out that several different philosophies underly much of the work. Upon talking to Dan

Scaffolding at the Bone House

or any of his workers, one realizes that the work of Friedrich Nietzsche, Plato, John Dewey, Jean-Paul Sartre, and Gestalt psychologists such as Max Wertheimer, Wolfgang Köhler, and Kurt Koffka has influenced the way that The Phoenix Commotion approaches its building projects.

First and foremost in the philosophy of The Phoenix Commotion is Friedrich Nietzsche's *The Birth of Tragedy*, a treatise that explains the tendency of Phillips and his workers to think outside of conventional building practices to create their structures. A pertinent section of *The Birth of Tragedy* explains the overall basis of Nietzsche's thought:

We shall have gained much for the science of aesthetics, once we perceive not merely by logical inference, but with the immediate certainty of vision, that the continuous development of art is bound up with the Apollonian and Dionysian duality—just as procreation depends on the duality of the sexes, involving perpetual strife with only periodically intervening reconciliations. The terms Dionysian *and* Apollonian *we borrow from the Greeks, who disclose to the discerning mind the profound mysteries of their view of art, not, to be sure, in concepts, but in the intensely clear figures of their gods. Through Apollo and Dionysus, the two art deities of the Greeks, we come to recognize that in the Greek world there existed a tremendous opposition, in origin and aims, between the Apollonian art of sculpture, and the nonimagistic, Dionysian art of music. (33)*[1]

T.J. Burdett & Sons Recycling

This short introduction to Nietzsche's work touches on most of what Dan Phillips derives from the work into his building practices. To further explain, the Apollonian tendency of the building industry is seen in the standard building practices that we see all around us. There are exact ways in which things are done: Houses should be square and level, windows should have no cracks in the glass, the roof of a porch should be level. Of course, reason dictates some of these practices. Structures should be level to make them easy to walk around in without being pulled by gravity in one direction or another. However, Dan points out to us that there is no particular reason why some things are standard-

Marissa Miller cuts a CD for the ceiling.

[1]**For more information, see *Basic Writings of Nietzsche*, Walter Kaufmann, ed. and trans. New York: The Modern Library, 2000.**

ized. For example, Dan dislikes drywall because it is merely a cheap, minimalist material. Why do most builders use it? Because it's cheap and standard. Most homebuyers expect drywall in their homes.

Broken granite forms a stack-wall in Burdett office buildihg.

Dan insists that we have become so entranced by the Apollonian side of building (and life in general) that we deny ourselves a vital part of human existence: the opposing, but essential, Dionysian aspect. To illustrate the way in which Dan and The Phoenix Commotion utilize this duality, one must look closely at some of the buildings the company has created. In the Victorian house, for example, Dan uses chicken eggs as architectural buttons on the turret of the house. Traditional practice dictates that one should use a more common material, such as wood, plastic, a type of stone, or marble for these decorative pieces.

However, the Dionysian tendency of art is to challenge the standards and to do something different. As in the two traditional modes of art described by Nietzsche, sculpture and music, the Apollonian perspective is constrained and more fixed while the Dionysian perspective is free, flowing, and fluid.

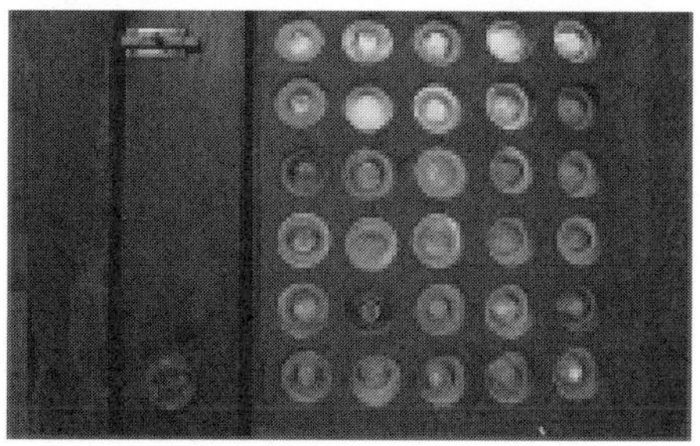

Wine-bottle butt window

Wall raising at Burdett office building

However, just as music is more than just random noises thrown together, we come to the next topic, the mantra of Dan and all of The Phoenix Commotion workers: that repetition creates pattern.

A blog entry from The Phoenix Commotion website demonstrates this concept in typical Dan Phillips and Phoenix Commotion fashion:

> *Repetition creates pattern. I have heard Dan Phillips say this mantra several times but I did not really understand it until I saw him give a short speech to some kids who had come to volunteer at a work site.*

Kristie Stevens' children designed a tile mosaic pattern in the family bathroom.

Dan looked around the work site and grabbed a handful of about 10 rocks of mortar that had been chipped off of old used bricks.

He placed the pieces of mortar in a pile, which looked like trash.

"When you look at this, what do you see?"

Various responses from the crowd.

Tile-shard shower by Paula McCullough

"A mess to clean up." Laughter.

"Junk."

"Yeah, but . . . ." He rearranged the pieces quickly like a magician into a circle. "What do you see now?"

In unison, "A circle."

Crew installing trusses

"Yes. We created a pattern out of junk, and everyone here can see it." He smiled.

"What if we take out one piece of mortar and replace it with . . . different stone?"

He grabs another stone of a different size and color and puts it in place of a piece of mortar.

Smither Park begins to take shape.

"What is it now?"

"A circle!" everyone shouts.

"Yup, still a circle. What about if I take out another piece of the mortar and replace it with a . . . stick?"

He does it quickly.

"Circle!"

"Yup, it's still a circle."

And today I got it, along with all the others. To use discarded items in design, without making your design look like "junk" you have to make a pattern that the eye can see.

Once you have established that pattern, you can even throw in a few odd pieces and still see the pattern. It doesn't look like "junk" because it is in harmony to a greater pattern.

Tile shards in a pattern of overlapping circles

What we see when we see "junk" is disharmony.

Good design creates a pattern that gets us to see the harmony, the cohesion of the pattern.

In fact, almost everything about the company seems to defy logic. Dan questions everything about the way human beings have come to regard housing. For example, he and his workers question how much living space a family actually needs. Just because there are four people in a family does not mean that every person needs his or her own room. However, in the American middle-class mindset, this is exactly what is expected. Dan admits that each person in a family would like to have his or her own personal space, but The Phoenix Commotion's solution to this is sleeping lofts, which are widely used in many of their later houses.

Smither Park sculpture evolving, by Kate Kendall

Burdett office building under construction

Dan explains that we have confused Maslow's hierarchy of needs by placing housing above more important things. Housing (shelter) is a lower-order need of human beings, according to Maslow's hierarchy, yet in much of the world today we see housing as a commodity or status symbol rather than shelter. We have inverted the pyramid, placing the basic physiological need for shelter above any true self-fulfillment, community, esteem, and love. Why do we do this? Dan claims that we are led to follow what the guy next door does because we want to compete for status. We see that the guy next door is building a house that's 2000 square feet. So we see our well-to-do neighbors building large houses, and we conclude that having a large house is what makes one successful.

Eric Farris decided to build his own house, sized modestly for himself and his wife and child, 380 square feet.

Central to The Phoenix Commotion's themes is the idea that we must all participate in our communities and give something back. The company and Phillips have accomplished this ideal in yet

Dan works on carving for Burdett building.

one more way in Huntsville, Texas: by helping to form the Trash into Plowshares ("TIP") warehouse in Huntsville in November 2003. The TIP warehouse is a two-sided structure that accepts donations from local builders and citizens.

At the TIP warehouse, customers complete a questionnaire and sign a liability waiver. The city also keeps track of the materials the recipients take from the warehouse. Because the warehouse is located at the same location as the transfer station, the city is able to weigh the quantities of materials, which helps them track inventory movement. The TIP warehouse accepts a variety of materials, such as plumbing and lighting fixtures, lumber, flooring, tile, windows, and doors.

Materials are donated by the bundle.

At the very least, Dan Phillips and The Phoenix Commotion have made the rest of the world notice that there is a different way to look at things, a different way to live. The following blog entry by Neko, a Phoenix Commotion employee and Homestead Initiative participant, sums up just what it means to be a part of the building community with Dan and the impact that it's having on the building industry one person at a time:

Dan & Neko Richardson

A Few Words About Building Community

Words I never wanted to text to anyone went to my next-door neighbor George last weekend.

"What would I do in the event that my cement slabs for my footings are not exactly level?"

The wait was painful as I imagined him laughing hysteri cally.

Josh's foundation

"That's no problem, you put dry concrete at the bottom of the footings to make sure they are level on all sides and shims at the top of the footings when you check for level the last time."

"Thanks George. "

"You're welcome."

Burdett roof takes shape.

Within a few minutes I got a response from Dan as well.

The text from Mr. Dan Phillips said, "I'm on my way over."

Dan came over to my lot on his day off just to make sure that I got my foundation right.

Yesterday Josh sent me a text letting me know he has extra lumber that I can have for my house.

"Is there a good time for me to come over and look at it?"

He responded, "Anytime you see my truck in the driveway."

I have only met Josh twice. He thought to offer me what he can.

Dan in the finished Tree House

Crew member Matt Gifford works on the Burdett logo from trash.

Bob and Edie live in the Bone House and have offered the use of their shop and tools.

Shannon has taught me carpentry with great patience and without laughing too much.

Matt has taught me about art and building.

Linda has taught me about mosaics and makes me laugh.

Dan has inspired all of us.

I feel very humbled to be in such good company and realize it's worth mentioning as you pick your community to build your place, that it's not just about the land. You need to have a community of builders that will support you with their experience.

After just a short time of building I have realized again and again that there is no way I could do this without them. Just when I think I have a solid plan, something always comes up that is unexpected.

Builders have been through it all and usually like to help each other. Don't think you can do this by yourself and even if you could, it would not be as good or as much fun, as with a community of builders.

I know I will never be able to return the kindness to all the people who have helped me and I am just beginning.

1323

The Victorian House

The Victorian House: The First Experiment

by Dustin Levien

As I had grown accustomed to my expectations, I had insensibly begun to notice their effect upon myself and those around me. Their influence on my own character, I disguised from my recognition as much as possible, but I knew very well that it was not all good. ~Charles Dickens, *Great Expectations*

Main living area with crossbeams

The Victorian House was the first of The Phoenix Commotion building projects, the first experiment that led to discoveries in Dan Phillips' way of thinking about what a house is and what it should be. Dan and his wife Marsha mortgaged their own home and cleared out their savings in order to buy the lot that the Victorian House sits on and the lot for the Budweiser House next door.

As Dan explained, the Victorian House was the beginning of his experimentation with construction. He already had an idea of the basic plan: recycled materials, unskilled workers, and innovative building practices, such as stacked construction using wooden blocks and chicken eggs as architectural buttons. From the beginning, he also planned to target the financially lower end of the population, such as single parents, low-income families, and struggling artists.

Skylight in main living area

Turret on outside of house

Inside view of the turret

Dan has accomplished all of these goals, but he had to learn as he experimented. He pointed out in one of our interviews that he learned of his own limitations and misconceptions during the construction of these early houses, just as he has on every house he has built

Turret

since. One of the main lessons that he learned was that he was a victim of the middle-class American mindset that dictated the size and space needed for a family home. The Victorian House is 1400 square feet, which is larger than most of The Phoenix Commotion houses. As of 2011, Dan strives to build homes no larger than 800 to 1000 square feet.

The home was inspired by the Painted Ladies Victorian homes in San Francisco. In 1978, a book about San Francisco's stunning Victorian homes introduced the rest of America to the style of Victorian houses painted in vibrant colors. The book is called *Painted Ladies*, and the name became synonymous with vividly colored reanimations of older Victorian homes. The authors of *Painted Ladies* used the following criteria for identifying the houses they included in their book:

Door frame

- *That the Victorian building be a balanced, felicitous blend of color and architecture*
- *That the house be painted in three or more contrasting colors.*
- *And that color be used to bring out the decorative ruffles and flourishes*[1]

It is no surprise that The Phoenix Commotion used the model of these rejuvenated houses for its first project. The whole idea behind the Painted Ladies movement is to breathe new life into old buildings, much in line with The Phoenix Commotion's purpose of breathing new life into old materials.

During this early experimentation, The Phoenix Commotion used a variety of materials in innovative ways. From the outside, the Victorian House looks like a fairly regular older home. However, upon closer examination of the outside and inside of the house, it is apparent that this is no ordinary Victorian home. Unlike a typical home, the house has no studs: The walls consist of six-by-six blocks of Western red cedar, one of the most expensive building materials available, purchased by The Phoenix Commotion from McMillan Bloedel—which

Stacked 6 X 6 cutoff construction

[1]For more information see *Daughters of Painted Ladies* by Elizabeth Pomada and Michael Larsen, New York: E.P. Dutton, 1987.

was later bought out by Weyerhaeuser—for $60 per 1000 board feet, a vast reduction over the market price of $1000 per 1000 board feet. The blocks are stacked like bricks and held together primarily with a construction adhesive called Liquid Nails, much as mortar is used to hold together bricks in a conventional brick wall. The Phoenix Commotion utilized 20-foot beams in the main living area for crossbeams to support the roof.

The house also features a two-person bathtub with spouts handcrafted of bois d'arc wood, also known as Osage Orange, one of the strongest woods available. Dan explains that he built a two-person bathtub because "it's not just a question of hygiene, but there's a possibility of recreation as well." The faucet is made out of a piece of Osage Orange, and Dan explains that "it looks a little phallic, but after all, it's a bathroom."

Handcrafted bois d'arc shower head

The double front door with a three-light transom is an "architectural antique," according to Dan, and the lockset itself is probably worth more than two hundred dollars. The door was headed for the landfill because it no longer conforms to standard sizes for door frames in America's standardized building industry.

The kitchen utilizes mostly recycled materials, including a 1952 O'Keefe & Merritt stove. Dan prefers to use recycled appliances if possible. However, if a home requires new appliances, he says that Energy-Star appliances are a must. He endeavors to reduce waste by using recycled materials in construction as well as reducing waste during occupancy.

A skylight allows natural light to enter the living areas.

Handcrafted tub

Dan explains that he no longer uses skylights in his houses because they are not energy efficient. The use of sunlight instead of electric light seems like a sound concept to most trying to conserve energy. However, Dan points out that the amount of heat let into the interior of the house through large skylights outweighs the conservation of energy by not using a light bulb. The Phoenix Commotion's solution to the need for natural light without the sacrifice of energy efficiency is using a solar tube. Many of the later houses, such as the Bone House, utilize solar tubes to let in natural light without allowing excessive heat to enter the interior space.

The staircase in the Victorian House is also recycled. Dan bought it for $20, including delivery to the jobsite. The turret

Kitchen with recycled appliances

is made from scrap nine-inch pieces of two-by- fours. Looking up into the turret from the inside, one sees that the edges of the walls are uneven because the scraps of two-by-fours do not make nice, soft edges. Dan explains that "if that ruins your life, then you shouldn't live there."

The house also features a laundry chute with an antique shoe last used as part of the handle. The owners of the home step on the shoe last, which opens the door on the laundry chute. The chute opens up right above the washing machine.

The architectural buttons on the corbels, located under the turret, are made out of chicken eggs. They serve a two-fold purpose, as do many of Dan's building materials. First, you have breakfast. Then you fill the eggs with Bondo, paint them, and nail them up for an aesthetically pleasing decoration at a fraction of the price. Hickory nuts are used in the stick-and-ball fretwork on the front entryway, another example of The Phoenix Commotion's ingenuity in using uncommon yet inexpensive building materials.

$20 Staircase

The Victorian house exemplifies The Phoenix Commotion's early ingenuity in using recycled materials to create beautiful, sustainable housing.

Laundry chute

Hickory nuts and chicken eggs become decorative buttons on the corbels supporting the turret.

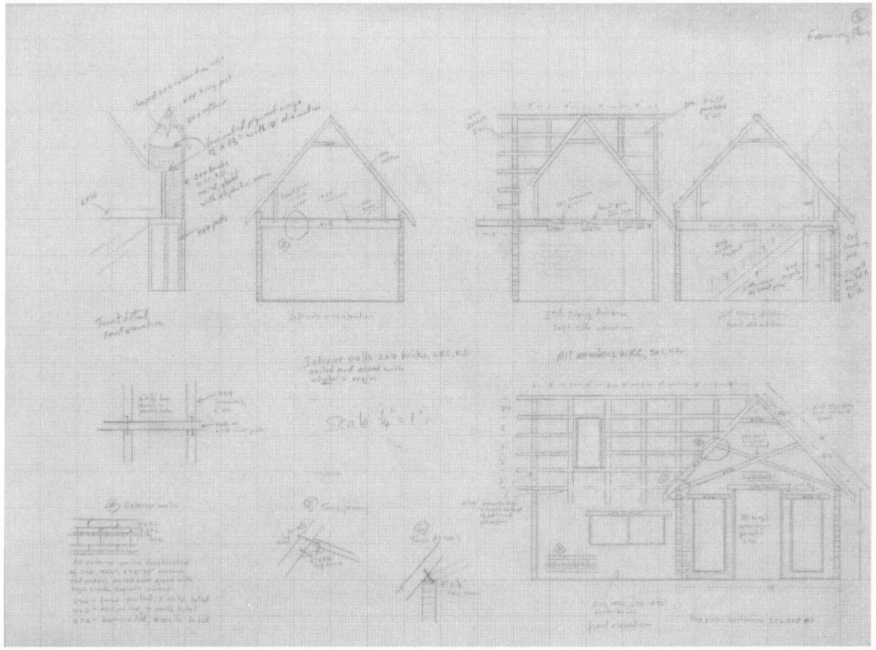

Initial sketch of Victorian House

Elevations of Victorian House

Dan looks down at the living room.

Hickory nuts in stick-and-ball fretwork

1321

The Budweiser House

The Budweiser House: Putting Size on the Radar

by Doug Haines

> *"Simplicity, simplicity, simplicity! I say, let your affairs be as two or three, and not a hundred or a thousand; instead of a million count half a dozen, and keep your accounts on your thumbnail . . . . Simplify, simply."*
>
> ~Henry David Thoreau

Even the Baptists call it the Budweiser House. Listed as a three-story boutique cottage, the Budweiser House, a towering monument to the American lager, is nestled snugly in the buckle of the East Texas Bible Belt. Based mostly on the label and not the can, the house also stands as a constant reminder to Dan Phillips of how quickly things can go awry in the absence of self-control.

His heart was in the right place. After completing his maiden voyage with the Victorian House, Dan was eager to start his next project. He soon decided that a hardworking employee with an ever-expanding family and an unwavering love for the best Anheuser-Busch has to offer would be the perfect candidate for the next Phoenix Commotion experiment in sustainable living. There were still flaws in the formula, but it often takes failure to achieve perfection. The Budweiser House had more than its share of failures.

Built in 2001, the house caused quite a stir within its conservative community, but eventually its unique style won the locals over. Weighing in at what Phillips considers a whopping 2,284 sq. ft., the Budweiser House offers 4 bedrooms, 2.5 bathrooms, a spacious eat-in kitchen, an office (or possibly an extra bedroom/apartment), and a loft with a balcony located

Dan during construction

directly above the master bedroom. With its exterior proudly flaunting the red, white, blue, and silver of the Budweiser coat-of-arms, this homage to hops and barley malt is full of subtle surprises and resourceful innovations in design. The bathrooms alone are works of art, both practical and ingenious. Though the house incorporates many of the stylistic quirks that make a Phillips home a Phillips home, it also embodies a lesson that Dan will not soon forget.

"Unfortunately, when you have free materials and cheap labor to work with, it's real easy to lose track of the road," Phillips told me one afternoon. We were sitting in the shade outside the T.J. Burdett and Sons Recycling Center under a sign that read, "I WANT YOUR CAN!" The irony was lost on no one. We were discussing what was wrong with the current

American middle-class mindset and how this house based on a beer label was the catalyst for so many revelations. The family it was intended for was already big, including four adults, a menagerie of pets, one small child, and another on the way. Size was not yet on Phillips' radar, and as he'd tried to accommodate the family, the house itself began to sprawl wildly out of control.

Budweiser posters used for papier-mâché ceiling

In today's society, there is a predisposition, with the exception of couples, that everyone in the house needs their own bedroom. Phillips has since learned that it is possible for everyone to have their own space without necessarily having their own room. Lofts have become a staple in the houses that The Phoenix Commotion builds. They conserve space while still providing a sense of sanctuary to the occupant. Especially for young children, lofts are the perfect answer to the question of how to best utilize whatever space is available. "They're every child's dream!" Phillips exclaimed with his own childlike enthusiasm.

Texture and whimsy adorn the gable wall.

The office, or fifth bedroom, was originally meant to be an additional source of income for the family. Set up to be its own apartment, the thinking was that they could rent it out and use the revenue to pay off the ridiculously low mortgage on the property. Unfortunately, when you've been living beneath the poverty line for as long as so many of The Phoenix Commotion's families have, there is a sense that one should pay it forward. Rather than renting the room out, it became a squatter's refuge and a wasted opportunity.

Design take-offs reminiscent of Budweiser can

Soon the family fell on hard times again and was forced to take out another loan. Without stellar credit, their options were limited, and the family fell prey to a predatory lender. Phillips describes the contract the owners signed as "a ream of paper full of legalese." When the subprime market collapsed, the interest rate on the loan was jacked up unmercifully to 13%. The owners were forced to default, and the lenders took over. The Budweiser House experiment was over. And as far as Phillips and The Phoenix Commotion were concerned, it had failed miserably.

Doorbell

The houses that have followed this project have progressively shrunk in size, but not

Shaper deadbolt

in ambition or ingenuity. By building smaller bedrooms and utilizing the loft concept, The Phoenix Commotion has since learned to make better use of limited space. Phillips now swears that he will never build another house over 1,000 sq. ft. This is less than half the size of the Budweiser House. Besides the additional time it takes to build a large house, there is also the loss of sustainability innate to such a structure. It becomes harder to clean, heat, and cool. It also becomes more difficult for the owner to sustain financially. Dan Phillips does not build houses for banks or for the people he refers to as "the gentry." He builds houses for people who need a little help in a difficult economy. He builds houses for people with more dreams than disposable income. The experience with the Budweiser House drove this message home for Phillips and The Phoenix Commotion. Sustainability and simplicity of life are key.

Beer Bottle Light Fixture

This is not to say that a Phoenix Commotion house is simplistic by any means. Besides sporting numerous Budweiser logos, stars, hops, and other details found on the self-proclaimed King of Beers label, the house is also full of inventive design features and details that only a master craftsman of Phillips' skill and creative nature could produce. Perhaps the handmade plaque found at the entrance of the house says it best, as it takes liberty with the Anheuser-Busch pledge:

Stained-glass side-lights

Papier-mâché ceiling

This is the famous Budweiser house. We know of no house produced by any other carpenter which takes so much time and patience. Our exclusive aftermarket aging produces a taste, a smoothness, and a livability you will find in no other house at any price.

Hops and barley

Creativity can have its price, too. The papier-mâché floors and ceilings made from old Budweiser 30-pack boxes, though initially aesthetically pleasing, turned out to be unable to endure the test of time. Due to traffic, the floors were the first to begin peeling, but the ceilings soon followed. The problem was that the sealing agent used to solidify them was unable to penetrate the thick, gloss-coated cardboard, an issue that Phillips has since corrected by leaving the agent on for a longer period of time and by using thinner

Re-write of the Budweiser pledge

Beer-box ceiling on porch

paper products in future homes.

Another Budweiser House experiment that has been discontinued in subsequent houses is the skylight. The concept of the skylight was to bring in more natural light, thus cutting down on the energy needed to light the home during the day. For this task, Phillips used some double-paned sliding glass doors that he had salvaged. Unfortunately, the skylights turned out to be inefficient as far as heating and cooling are concerned, therefore negating their usefulness in energy conservation.

Sliding glass door skylight

Still fond of natural light, Phillips has since traded the skylight for the more efficient alternative of solar tubes (or sun scopes), which do basically the same thing lighting-wise, but without the sizable exposure to the elements. By using broken mirror glass to create the reflective surface, the homemade solar tubes that The Phoenix Commotion now installs in their homes is an incredibly clever and inexpensive solution to this problem.

Kitchen: granite coutertops and beer-box floor

With its salvaged stained-glass windows and granite countertops, the Budweiser House did have its successes. Its attention to detail is amazing, and the house is full of secret compartments that its new owners will probably never be fully aware of. Today, Phillips describes it as a "wonderful house that taught me the importance of wrangling in a project when it begins to sprawl." He is particularly proud of the bathrooms he created in the home, each unique and beautiful.

Barley-hops design in cornice detail

The downstairs bathroom features a tub/shower built to give the impression of a glass of beer. The white tile he used, a Dumpster treasure, includes a series of Budweiser bottle caps rising up to represent the bubbles of a freshly poured draft.

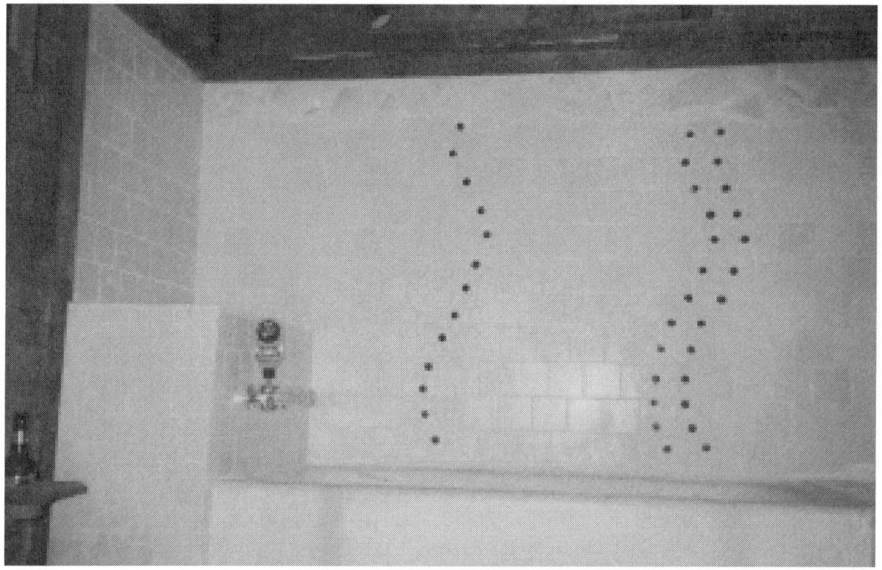

Downstairs bathroom

The shower fixture is an actual Budweiser tap, and the toilet-paper dispenser a Budweiser bottle. The upstairs bathroom also utilizes the white marble tiles Phillips and his crew found discarded in a Dumpster outside a cookie-cutter mini-mansion.

Junkyards, trash bins, recycling centers, and garage-sale leftovers provide The Phoenix Commotion with the majority of their materials. "It's just like Home Depot, only you have to be a little more creative and think outside the box," Phillips says with a knowing grin.

A repurposed entry-hall chandelier hangs brilliantly above the tub in the upstairs bathroom, adding a strange touch of class and creating a one-of-a-kind bathroom experience for all who enter. Even the half bath in the Budweiser House is unique. Its rustic walls are built out of more discarded wood and the floors from expensive broken tiles that were donated to the project. Some other interesting features of this half bath include the urinal, the bidet, and a pedestal from a birdbath that Phillips has turned into a toilet paper roll holder.

Though the Budweiser House experiment did not turn out exactly as Phillips and The Phoenix Commotion had envisioned, it stands as a valuable lesson learned to all who were involved.

"It put size on my radar," explained Phillips, who has now learned that free materials and low- cost labor do not excuse excess. In order to create truly sustainable living, one must downsize the American dream and embrace a simpler way of living.

Upstairs bathroom

1321

Half bath

Designs from the can mounted under the eaves

House tucked back among trees

The Ranch House

The Ranch House: A Bois D'arc Bounty

by Jake Gebhardt

Dan Phillips' unique designs and ingenious use of materials in home construction have graced Huntsville, Texas, with many fascinating houses that continue to turn heads today. Nestled away in the neighborhoods of Huntsville is a group of four houses that are as interesting as they are unique. From the fairytale-like appeal of the Storybook House to the gleaming roof of the License Plate House, Dan's projects fascinate both locals and outsiders alike. One of the more subtle houses in this group of Phoenix Commotion constructions is the rus-

Early Ranch House construction

tic Ranch House. This wooden house stands as a country-style example of Dan's ingenious design and creative use of spare materials.

The Ranch House might not be as flashy as some of the neighboring Phoenix Commotion houses, but its soul and appeal are pure Texan. This house's rustic, down-home appearance instantly reminds many visitors of the ranch-style houses of the Texas countryside. Most of the house is made from wood, specifically Western Red Cedar and bois d'arc. Instantly, visitors' eyes are drawn to the porch because of its gnarly look. Here, Dan opted to use bois d'arc for the support columns and railing. This super-hard, disease-resistant wood takes quite a bit more work to get right in construction, but since the material was freely available, it became a staple element in several areas of the house. Normally, this type of wood would be ill-suited for construction projects. Even in the Ranch House, only certain projects could use bois d'arc because of its uneven, knotty surface. However, Dan was able to turn this difficulty into a unique opportunity for the project.

Ranch House interior, main staircase

The rustic ranch style continues as you walk into the house. The most prominent structure, the stairway to the second floor, immediately stands out. A large, thick bois d'arc trunk is used for the support structure running along the bottom side of the stairway. This trunk snakes its way from the floor of the first story nearly to the floor of the second story. Smaller branches are then used for the balusters, supporting the smaller part of the bois d'arc trunk that functions as the railing for the stairs. This central feature makes the house come alive, with the stair rail seemingly growing out of the ground, through the floor, and up to the second floor of the house.

Further emphasizing the wooden nature of the house is the material used for the interior walls. Blocks of Western Red Cedar are used in place of drywall. Since the wood used was donated from other projects, it is in various sizes. Normally, uneven building materials can cause some construction issues. However, Dan looked at this as an opportunity, fitting the various sizes of wood together to form a solid, patterned wall. This design might not be uniform or perfect, but it adds soul and character to the house. After all, a typical old-style ranch house probably wouldn't be made of perfect, pre-fabricated materials.

Furthermore, by using discarded and unusual construction materials, Dan and The Phoenix Commotion are able to practice greener, more sustainable building practices. In addition to assuring sustainability, buildings designed by The Phoenix Commotion are typically smaller-sized houses. The Ranch House is no different. However, houses designed by Dan Phillips are not *too* small. In the Ranch House, the rustic design combines with the smaller-sized footprint to create a warm atmosphere suited for families of all sizes. Most important, this smaller design lends itself well to sustainable building practices favored in all of Dan Philips' projects.

Ranch House interior stairs

Sustainability is what will allow this country to move toward a successful future. Unless building methods are modified to keep sustainability in mind, it will become more and more difficult to maintain a middle-class American lifestyle. Although certain sacrifices need to be made to better use the remaining resources we have, people do not have to give up everything. A bit of thought and planning ahead of time will not only save money later but will also help to maintain the environment for future generations. Dan's designs emphasize this practice, helping to create affordable housing that is sustainable in both construction and living.

The Ranch House began a transition from previous larger building projects to smaller, more sustainable and manageable building practices. From the beginning, Dan's projects have emphasized sustainability and material efficiency. However, even with cheap materials and labor, a sustainable house can

Completed Ranch House (Front)

become an overwhelming logistical nightmare, as was the case with some of his earlier houses. By shifting to a smaller design, sustainability is better maintained, and construction becomes significantly easier. This shift in design concept resulted in a focus that continues in Dan's houses today. By downsizing overall square footage and better utilizing the existing floor plan, material, labor, and costs are easier to manage. Additionally, the Ranch House continued to expand the types of materials that Dan used in his houses. Sustainable and renewable materials have been a cornerstone of Dan Phillips' and The Phoenix Commotion's building projects. What sets these houses apart is how materials are used, especially when those materials are unconventional.

What stands out about the Ranch House's design and construction is the significant use of renewable materials. Much of the house is made of wood, and several different types of wood are used in its construction. One of the materials described earlier that adds a significant visual appeal to the Ranch House is bois d'arc. Normally, a Texas citizen might look at this material as very difficult to work with. Bois d'arc is a very hard, very gnarly tree indigenous to Central and East Texas, and it is difficult to cut and process. While this hardness might be considered a plus for durability, the tree does not grow in an easy-to-harvest form. Instead, it grows large, undisciplined branch structures ill-suited for most construction projects. Whereas most builders might see natural, winding branches as a setback in construction, Dan saw them as an opportunity. Although this wood would be inappropriate to use in plank-style construction, it has a nearly unbeatable potential for decorative and minor structural uses. Since the shapes are so unusual, many of the joints and connections for this wood have to be custom made. While the steps or planks of the house might be made of a more typical wood, the gnarly nature of bois d'arc allows for the tree to be used in a unique and rustic design. Dan was able to use this material to add character to the Ranch House while maintaining the required strength and durability necessary for any construction project. With minimal standard maintenance, this wood looks rustic, feels natural, and can potentially last a lifetime.

As useful as bois d'arc was in the construction of the Ranch House, several other wood types were needed to com-

Early Ranch House construction

plete the project. Part of Dan's philosophy is to use whatever happens to be available. Since he builds only wooden houses, any wood out there is fair game. Everything from quality and expensive types of wood to leftover scraps were used in the construction. Where bois d'arc was inappropriate, Dan and The Phoenix Commotion crew would use whatever supplies were available at the time. Since Dan had a lot of Western Red Cedar on hand, he chose to use it extensively in the construction of the Ranch House. This spare Western Red Cedar gave rise to the design of the walls used in the house, one of its key features. Even if something isn't ideal for a construction project, The Phoenix Commotion will try to use it.

Vaulted ceiling in Ranch House

Dan gives Donna Zuniga a tour.

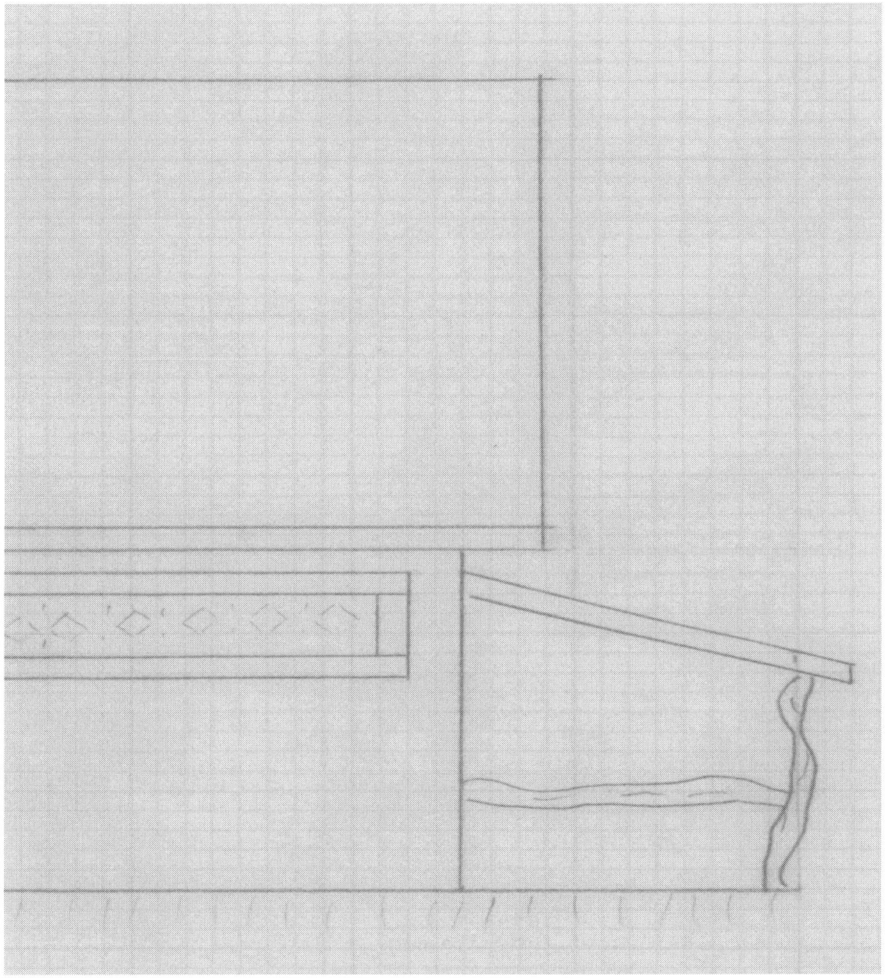

Early Ranch House sketch (side)

In addition to Western Red Cedar, other woods, such as Southern Yellow Pine and engineered wood products, were used when available. If Dan and The Phoenix Commotion had larger pieces of wood donated to them, these larger, post-like materials could then potentially be used for heavier structural purposes.

Dan is often able to obtain materials that, although they have slight imperfections, will still work perfectly for other construction purposes. Damaged expensive tile can be turned into a grouted mosaic design for a floor or countertop. Left-over end cuts of wood or sun-bleached wood that no longer looks perfect can be used in housing construction, either for design or for structural purposes. By using these materials that would normally be thrown away, Dan and The Phoenix Commotion are able to promote a better and more sustainable construction environment. Not only are the materials cheaper, but less waste is created because nearly everything is used.

Even if discarded materials are used in the construction of the house, structures built by The Phoenix Commotion are still designed to last a lifetime. This does not mean that zero maintenance is required for the houses. In order to keep a

Completed Ranch House porch

structure in a livable state, minor repairs still need to be performed. If issues are addressed as they arise, then the house could easily last for several generations.

If small things are left to grow and fester into larger problems, families can encounter issues that will require significant work to fix. Whereas a rustic-style house like the Ranch House might show wear and tear less obviously than a more traditional house, it still has to be taken care of. Most of the maintenance can be performed by the homeowner. Additionally, Dan often offers help to residents who live in houses designed by him, empowering home owners with the necessary skills and training to keep their houses in good repair.

A final unique aspect of the Ranch House is the people who live there. Dan and The Phoenix Commotion focus their efforts on populations in need. Often, people who originally live in houses built by The Phoenix Commotion are low-income families, artists, or similar people in need. Because of the volatile nature and risk involved with building and financing a house for these at-risk groups, sometimes things do not turn out perfect for every owner of a house built by Dan and The Phoenix Commotion. However, the Ranch House, built for Bobby and Earnest Carter, is one of their success stories. This generous, hard-working family deserved to have a shot at homeownership, and Dan was able to provide them an opportunity. Bobby and Earnest Carter are a testament to Dan Phillips' and The Phoenix Commotion's philosophy. Not only are they trying to create a sustainable building environment, but they are there to give jobs to hard-working people and opportunities to those who otherwise would not enjoy them.

Beyond sustainability, the ultimate goal of Dan Phillips and The Phoenix Commotion is to meet the needs of the people who truly deserve to have a chance. With a bit of compromise and change, any person can live in a house built by The Phoenix Commotion. However, it takes a visionary like Dan

Dan after another day's hard work

to make such unique houses for people in the Huntsville community. By providing an opportunity to deserving families, Dan Phillips and The Phoenix Commotion are able to serve the Huntsville community and significantly contribute to the idea of sustainable, responsible construction practices.

The License Plate House

The License Plate House: Adapt and Overcome

By Christina Fernandez

"Houses are built to live in, and not to look on: therefore let use be preferred before uniformity." ~Francis Bacon

No one has ever questioned the creativity behind Dan Phillips and The Phoenix Commotion vision. Over the years, Dan and his crew have proved themselves to be masters of creating beauty and function out of what others have discarded. Unfortunately, the banks have not always trusted the practicality of all his initial designs. For instance, the house that has come to be known as the License Plate House was originally designed to look like an old boot, paying homage to Mother Goose's famous nursery rhyme, "There Was an Old Woman Who Lived In a Shoe." According to Dan, he had started out with the idea to build a geodesic dome for the toe of the boot, "which would then yield to standard framing with applique for the top and a circular pitched roof and stucco on the outside," a concept that Dan still feels holds potential.

Front wall is 18" thick.

After receiving "a magnificent loan package" for his three upcoming projects from a Dallas lender, Dan's local bank, which was acting as the "fiduciary and administer of the loan," rejected the designs for the three houses, including the Shoe House. The bank's fear was that if the owners were to default on the loan, then a shoe-shaped house might be a difficult resell in a struggling housing market. The news came as a surprise to Phillips, who now found himself forced to come up with all new ideas and layouts for the three houses in one night. Luckily, he had help from his wife, Marsha, who drew up the blueprints and floor plans for the License Plate House that evening.

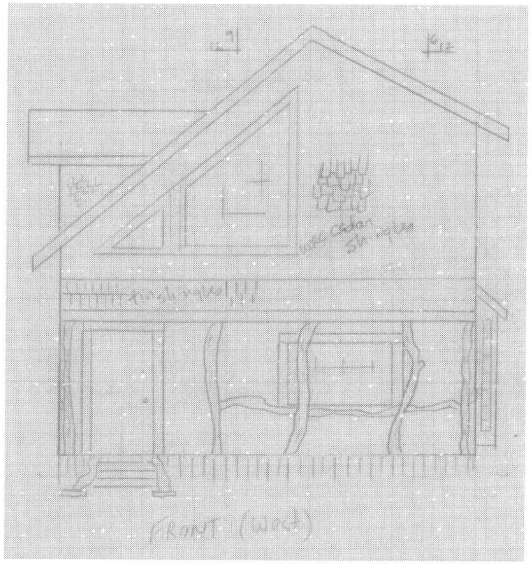

Marsha's early sketch of License Plate House

Impressed with his wife's concept, Dan followed through with the plans, making only minor changes to Marsha's design. Many of these changes were due to the lack of availability of certain materials and also to improve overall "jobsite expedience." He also decided to tweak the shape of the windows surrounding the house. For example, the one near the foot of the stairs was very wide but extremely short in height, barely giving a glimpse of the outside world—unacceptable for creating natural light within the home.

The pressure of devising all new plans for the three houses that followed The Ranch House in a midnight rush was no easy task, but the final product of the combined efforts of Dan and Marsha paid off in the end by creating three of the Phoenix Commotion's most notable houses: the License

Bottle caps used as shoe cleaner

Plate House, the Story Book House, and the Charleston House.

From a distance, the roof of the License Plate House looks like any other: shingled and plain. However, if someone were to take a closer look from either side of the roof, the

License plates make a dandy roof.

difference would quickly become apparent. Rather than using the fiberglass shingles found on most houses today, the Phillips crew layered old discarded license plates over one another to create an extremely durable, practical, and one-of-a-kind roof built to stand up to whatever the Texas weather can deliver. Applying the same protective coating that is used on license plates to prevent corrosion during manufacturing (which Dan refers to as "silvery coating"), the Phoenix Commotion crew managed to make the roof even more impervious to the elements. Besides the roof's durability, the reflectivity of the license plates helps to keep the interior of the house cooler during brutally hot Texas summer days.

Wood-shingled siding

The front porch is decorated with intricate designs, such as a blue snake with orange stripes and a flower, a mosaic that the Phoenix Commotion crew created by using beer bottle caps as their medium.

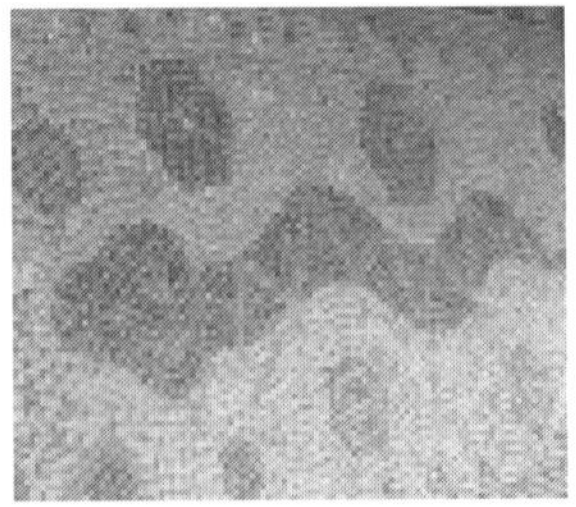

Bottle-cap snake mosaic

Upon entering the License Plate House, one notices that there is a continuation of the shingled look of the exterior sheathing, which is made of Western Red Cedar. Inside, the license plate theme continues. In one of the bedrooms, over seventy hand-picked plates have been plastered and displayed in one long strip along the ceiling. Dan and the crew chose plates that they found interesting, such as "COW-BOY,"

Bedroom ceiling with hand-picked plates

"FREAK I," and "WYATT." Other plates were chosen because of where they had come from, like a fertilizer truck, or because of whom they had once belonged to. For example, there are several plates that were once owned by Texas state judges. And some plates were chosen because of a message or statement that the previous owners had felt the need to advertise, like "Keep Texas Wild."

The rooms within the License Plate House, including the kitchen, are all very small but cozy, giving the interior a "homey" feel. The kitchen cabinets have a unique appearance due to the reddish colored wood referred to as Oriented Strand Board (OSB), which is displayed in the middle of each cabinet. The outer edges of the cabinets were constructed of Western Red Cedar. Meanwhile, the kitchen ceiling is decorated with strips of ¼-inch plywood laid over white papier-mâché, and the floor was made by carefully laying out various shades and colors of discarded granite.

Dan in the kitchen

The stairs in The License Plate House are also unique. On the way up, one immediately notices that the bannister is held up by wide, ragged-looking wooden boards, which lack any kind of uniformity.

Bathroom Vanity

The next notable room in the house is the bathroom. There are three large lightbulbs slanted over the sink, bringing to mind a celebrity's dressing room vanity. Beautiful in its simplicity, the bathroom ceiling is covered with varying rectangles, as well as some irregular shapes placed randomly against the clustered pieces of mirror. It was in this bathroom that Dan first experimented with mirror shards. Both the bottle cap and the mirror-shard designs originated with this house, and it is an experiment that Dan has continued to work with in his other projects.

The construction of each Phoenix Commotion house depends upon the materials that are available at the time. This gives each home its own personality. In Texas, Huntsville is known for two main things: its exceptional Criminal Justice program at Sam Houston State University and its prison system, where prisoners make thousands of license plates each day. This is why the License Plate House is so unique to this part of the state. In fact, Dan knows of no other like it in the country.

Andrew, one of the owners, seems very pleased with his home and appreciates the uniqueness of living in a one-of-a-kind house. However, he did admit that it took a while to get used to it. He loves the fact that the house helps him save money on his electricity and water bills. For example, the tankless hot water heater is extremely efficient and reliable. Even if the power were to go out, the house would still have water. Andrew also takes great pride in knowing that his house is made from recycled materials and is a part of the sustainable living movement that Dan and his crew have helped to create in such an unlikely place—East Texas.

Entryway & Bannister

Despite its rough beginnings, the late-night plans that Dan and Marsha Phillips came up with to replace what was to be the Shoe House have proved to be a success. The License Plate House projects an understanding of the need to reuse, rather than discard, without ever sacrificing style for sustainability. Built in less than eight months, the house was completed in April of 2003 and stands as a monument to Dan and The Phoenix Commotion's ability to adapt and overcome.

The Storybook House

<u>The Storybook House</u>: To Live in a Fairy Tale

By Amanda Dellett

If one were to make his way along the sleepy, meandering streets of Huntsville, he might eventually find himself face-to-face with a house that looks as if it came straight out of *Grimm's Fairy Tales*. The Storybook House, as it was eventually named, has come to represent the child-like imagination in all of us. This could have been the house that Little Red Riding Hood discovered while on her way to deliver food to her sick grandmother. Or perhaps this was the house Hansel and Gretel stumbled across when looking for shelter in the woods. Despite being less than a decade old, it has that old-world feel that tricks you into thinking that it has been nestled in that spot for generations. The Storybook House brings fantasy to reality and implores children and adults alike to recall their favorite stories.

Cat-slide roof over front door

Dan Phillips and The Phoenix Commotion didn't have a particular fable in mind when laying out the plans for this home, but it turned out magical nonetheless. Perhaps the most striking exterior feature is the roof, with its steeper-than-average pitch and gently waving striped pattern designed to simulate the thatched roofs seen on 16th-Century German, French, and English homes. The frumpy look of the house is intentional—two walls on the first floor have been slanted inward so that they are three degrees out of plumb. The second story is cantilevered over the first story by 24 inches, adding more square footage while also reenforcing that old-world feel. And, of course, no storybook house would be complete without dutch doors, diamond-mulioned windows, and a cat-slide roof over the front door.

Framed stained-glass window

The whimsical nature of the exterior is carried inside through the use of exposed beams and built-in shelves in the living and dining area. There is also a little nook on the upstairs landing that is secluded with its own small, round window. Altogether the home has three bedrooms and one-and-a-half baths. The three bedrooms are small, yet cozy, and have their own closets. One of the bedrooms has a sleeping loft. The front bedroom appears more spacious due to the very high ceiling and built-in shelving. The half-bathroom downstairs is also a laundry room, with a laundry chute coming from the bathroom above it. The upstairs bathroom mirror is a mosaic created out of broken shards of older mirrors that may have otherwise been thrown away. Pine floors run throughout the whole house with the exception of the kitchen, which is instead composed of a tile mosaic.

Diamond-mullioned windows complete Storybook theme.

Mirror and tile are just two of the materials that Dan says The Phoenix Commotion receives by the truckload. Both are often replaced by owners if they become cracked or otherwise damaged, and with tile especially, inventories are constantly being rotated, with some styles being discontinued. This ensures that there will always be a steady supply that can be used for other purposes. And the good news is that they don't even necessarily have to match.

One of Dan's most popular mantras is that "repetition creates pattern," a concept his wife taught him early on. In other words, two sets of tile with clashing patterns may not look that great if you lay one half of a room with one style and lay the other half of the room with the other. An average person would look at the room and be bothered by contrasting design. But if the two styles are laid in alternating patterns like stripes or a checkerboard, there is peace of mind. So why not take broken mirror shards or tile and create a mosaic out of them? It will result in an end product that is just as aesthetically pleasing as anything you can find in a high-end store; and on top of that, it's practically free. Another example of repetition creating pattern in the home can be found in the stained-glass window located in the top half of the Dutch door in the kitchen. It was designed by taking the butts of several different-colored wine bottles, arranging them in an eye-pleasing pattern, and then mounting them with stiff wire and mortar.

The house uses a gas pack as its main heating and cooling system. However, Dan claims that this decision was made back in the days when he didn't know any better. The more recent houses built by the company are designed so that a single window-unit will circulate air throughout the whole house. Nevertheless, the house is practical in other ways—there is a water catchment system in place that utilizes rainwater for toilet flushing and clothes washing. The house also uses a tankless water heater to cut down on energy costs.

The majority of the building materials for the house are repurposed. For example, the first story is timber-frame construction, the beams having been acquired from a local rancher who had them left over from his own house. At the time, Dan was still in the business of restoring antiques. The rancher contacted him about restoring a secretary, and the beams were payment for the work.

The second story of the house is framed with Southern Yellow Pine that was previously used as protectors between stacks of trailers loaded on an eighteen-wheeler. It was donated by Countryside Tailer Sales, a local trailer company. Weyerhaeuser of Houston donated the cedar cutoffs that were used for the decking of the roof, the cat-slide roof over the front door (2x6 and 2x8, respectively), and both Dutch doors (4x6). The Hardi-Board for the sheathing of the exterior was also acquired by way of Weyerhaeuser. They put Dan in contact with Hope Lumber Company, who was more than willing to give him two eighteen-wheeler loads of a discontinued dimension.

In fact, during this period of The Phoenix Commotion's history a lot of contacts were made either through word of mouth or by a growing presence in the media. The four diamond-mullioned windows were recovered from a demolition project of a Victorian house in Houston. A man named Mike McCorkle was renovating the home and read about Dan and The Phoenix Commotion in *Fine Homebuilding Magazine.*

Vintage door knocker

The unusual protruding stained-glass window on the first story was donated by a church through a man named John Fowler. Of course, some materials were also purchased, either because they had to be (like the trusses of the roof and the stucco that was troweled over the exterior) or because they were something special that went beautifully with the design (such as the doorknocker that Dan stumbled upon in an architectural antique salvage yard in Chicago while visiting their daughter).

In regards to the construction of the house, Dan was able to provide details on one of the most striking features: the roof. The trusses were purchased new, but appliqué was added on the bottom and top to give the impression of a ridgepole that had sagged for over 300 years. The Western Red Cedar cutoffs donated by Weyerhaeser for the decking are 2x6 to accommodate the swag. The rafter tails consist of 2x12 WRC cut into circles and mounted to each rafter. Then 1x2 WRC was nailed around each circle to give the curved appearance of the eaves. The shingles are an accumulation of leftover bundles from roofers; hence the multiple colors. Their arrangement in waving stripes adds animation to the fantastical design.

Shingles woven to simulate thatched roof

Finished in 2004, the house was originally designed as a spec house. The first owner was Ruth Bryant, a former member of the English Department at Sam Houston State University, who bought it for her great-niece to live in while in college. Over time the house came under new ownership and Matthew Ruffin, our director's son, was privileged to live there for roughly a year beginning in June of 2006. He claims that the house was a favorite hangout spot among his friends. They would put up strobe lights and have big dance parties, or they would hang out and eat and drink on the back porch with the Dutch door open so that they could talk to people in the dining/kitchen area.

Surely, living in a house that stands out from all of the others in the neighborhood will attract strangers. According to Matt, people weren't always forward enough to actually knock on the door, but on rare occasions that it did happen, the tenants were more than happy to give a tour. For the most part, people seemed to be content just driving by slowly to get a good look. Matt recalled how sometimes he would get freaked out if he was on the porch and saw someone driving by at 3 mph with their neck strained, that is, until he remembered that they were most likely ogling the house, not him.

Homes are kind of like a good storybook: You read it once and love it, but it's the second or third reading before you truly begin to appreciate the literature and all that it entails—the new details that you uncover, the feelings and ideas that stay with you and stir in your mind, and the methodical way the creator of the story lays the words upon the page and invites you to read between the lines. Likewise, there are some things about any house that are often missed at first glance by people doing a quick tour, but are noticed and appreciated by people that are honored to stay there for a period of time. One of Matt's favorites was the way the light would shine through the wine-bottle butts in the stained-glass window in the kitchen, displaying a rainbow of colors. Another was a special nook in the wall that was adorned on all three sides by windows. This was a great place for his potted plants in the winter.

The average person touring the house probably has no idea what it is like to live in a house that utilizes a tankless water heater and a water catchment system, but Matt explained that he barely even noticed. In fact, the only time he did notice was when someone would drop something between the floorboards of the porch (which he said happened often) and he'd have to navigate his way under the house, passing the cistern.

Stairway to back yard

As for the heating and cooling system, it is interesting how the upper level of the home stayed warm even with central A/C (although not that surprising, considering the Texas summers). Matt occupied a bedroom on the upper level, and he said he made it comfortable by regulating the air flow with fans.

The Storybook House has become an integral part of the character of Huntsville with its whimsical and majestic design. The fact that it was built at very low cost from materials that would have otherwise made their way to the landfill only adds to the appreciation felt by the community and the people that have been privileged enough to live there. Matt recalled that one of his favorite things to do was to find an interesting place to sit and just stare at the architecture from different angles, like the beams or the slant of the roof. According to him, it's not every day you get to go home and think "Dang, it's so cool that I live here," and I doubt anyone else who is lucky enough to live in one of Dan's homes will disagree.

Bench built by crew member

Dan examines framework of Storybook House

912

The Charleston House

The Charleston House: An Eclectic Sanctuary

by Anna Raye Jennings

"The house of every one is to him as his castle and fortress."
~Sir Edward Coke

Anyone who strolls down University Avenue in Huntsville, Texas, will notice two unusual houses situated side by side: the whimsical Storybook House and its fortress-like neighbor, the Charleston House. The observer might never guess that both houses owe their existence to The Phoenix Commotion, since they bear no resemblance to each other from the outside. The Storybook House, with its otherworldly appearance, might command the attention of onlookers until their eyes shift to the left and find the Charleston House, beautiful in its austerity. Its cedar planking, courtyard walls, and wrought-iron gate give it a character of dignity, but a closer look reveals lighthearted, eclectic features and salvaged materials that mark it unmistakably as a Phoenix Commotion creation.

Courtyard gate

As Dan Phillips planned the house, he found inspiration in the houses of Charleston with enclosed courtyards built for privacy. With this vision in mind, he led Phoenix Commotion in building a 3-bedroom, 1 ½-bathroom house with an enclosed courtyard. Dan endeavored to give it the charm of the houses he had seen in Charleston. However, the courtyard's wrought-iron gate evokes images of New Orleans architecture, since it came from that city. Mike McClorkle, a friend of Dan's, donated the gate, along with a matching balcony, knowing that Dan could find a use for them.

The antique front door was derelict until Dan found a new purpose for it in this house. Ordinarily, he avoids painting parts of his houses because this introduces decades of maintenance. However, an antique door is likely to have lead paint on it. When examining such a door, a health inspector will ask if it has lead paint and possibly even test it for lead. Dan, having no desire to wrangle with the health inspectors, remarked that his crew probably had to strip the door. Since he loves the color "pumpkin," he used that color to repaint this door and the French door leading to the patio. He also created house numbers to match that color.

The balcony

Not only did the Charleston House give salvaged treasures a second life, but it gave Dan an opportunity to experiment with materials that were piling up at his shop. Early on, it was called the Panel House because it was built entirely from 4′ x 8′ panels that Dan had constructed in the shop—floor panels, wall panels, and roof panels. As he designed the house, he sketched floor plans of how these panels would fit together, later transporting them to the building site. The crew laid the foundation, set up the wall panels, and added roof panels. It was the first time he had used this technique to build a house. Unfortunately, the panels did not fit together perfectly. He explained that new lumber does not always fit, so it is often necessary to make adjustments. He had to retrofit the panels, and it was a grueling process. Dan declared that he never wanted to build a house that way again, and he would rather put together materials on site from then on. Nonetheless, he and his crew managed to close the frame in only two days.

The house under construction

The Charleston House gained another nickname, the Cedar Plank House, because of its outer covering of cedar shingles. Both inside and outside the house, Dan used Western Red Cedar donated to him by Weyerhaeuser, a Houston wholesale lumber company that had accumulated piles of unsellable two-foot cedar boards. Dan explained that lumber ordinarily comes in standard dimensions scaled in two-foot increments: eight-foot boards, ten-foot boards, twelve-foot boards, and so on. Sometimes, a lumber company trims pieces from these boards in order to meet customer orders. For example, if a client orders eight-foot boards and that size happens to be out of stock, the company supplies the order by trimming longer boards. A lumber company may also accumulate scrap lumber when a client returns unused lumber to the company for a refund. By the time the customer returns them, the boards may have turned grey from weathering, as cedar is wont to do. Because of situations like this, Weyerhaeuser began supplying Dan with this scrap lumber, initially selling it to him for $100 per thousand feet. Eventually, they accumulated so much that they began shipping it to him for free instead of hauling it to the landfill, where they would have to pay tipping fees.

Early blueprints of Charleston House

The floors of the Charleston House are among its most interesting and beautiful aspects. In a downstairs bedroom, Dan created a hand-grained parquet floor from Western Red Cedar. He would place a 4′ x 4′ cedar board on a table and use a miter saw to trim off a wafer of the wood. Once he had accumulated enough wafers, he glued them to the floor, grouted them, and sealed them. This technique gave the flooring durability and an appealing visual texture.

For a downairs nook, which could function as a den or small office space, Dan made a cork floor. Cork flooring, normally laid down in sheets of cork, often costs $5 per square

Stairs in the living room

foot because homeowners prize it for its beauty and the pleasant tactile sensation of walking on it. However, Dan made this one for free from wine corks. One of these corks, in fact, came from an $1800 bottle. After Dan put out the word that he needed corks for one of his projects, people began donating them.

Many of the corks came from total strangers. Sometimes people gave the corks to him one at a time, as when an elderly lady placed one in his hand. Other times, someone would present him with an entire bucket filled with corks and instruct him not to tell anyone where they'd come from. Dan spent only about $20 on the floor, and that cost came from other materials he used for it: thin-set mortar, pre-mixed ceramic tile adhesive, glue, grout, and urethane. He put together the floor first by troweling down ceramic-tile adhesive and pushing the corks into it.

Parquet flooring

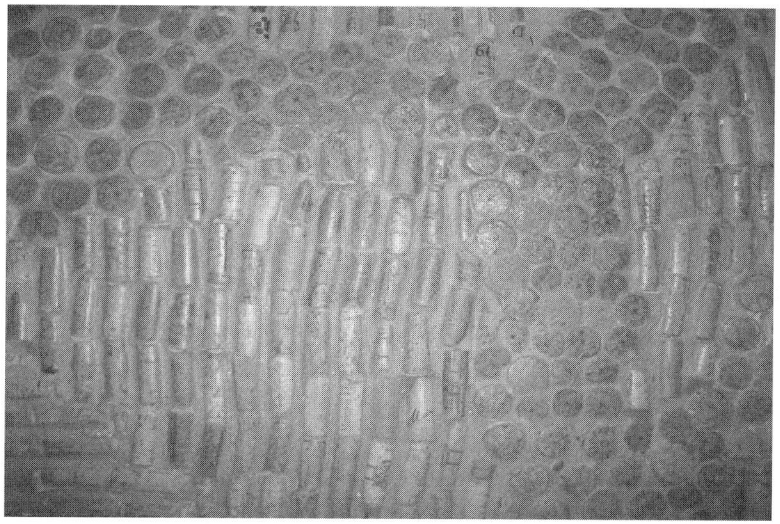

Close-up of cork flooring

He laid most of the corks down lengthwise but stood the champagne corks up because they were larger. For this reason, the champagne corks appear round. Because Dan finds symmetry "terrifying," he arranged the corks in an asymmetrical pattern and put a trim nail in each one to secure it in place. Afterward, he covered the corks with more tile grout and used muriatic acid to clean off the haze after it dried. This technique worked so well that it is still possible to read the writing on the corks.

The tiles on the living room and kitchen floor follow a checkerboard pattern: neutral-colored tiles with a mosaic intervention made of tile fragments. The neutral tiles do not match each other perfectly, but an observer would have to look closely to notice because the mosaic tiles take center stage. "Repetition creates unity," Dan explained. "The whole aesthetic constellation has to work." The countertops have the

Grapevine pattern in the cork flooring

Kitchen floor tiles

same checkerboard tile pattern as the living room and kitchen floors, but on a smaller scale: 6-inch instead of 12-inch. Dan added that there is no reason for tile to go into a landfill. Sometimes, wholesale tile companies accumulate it in their warehouses and contact him to let him know that they have some for free. Dan doesn't mind if it's broken, since he uses the broken bits in mosaics.

A doorway at the back of the kitchen leads to a bathroom where Eric Farris, a member of The Phoenix Commotion, created more mosaic tile designs on the floor. Another unusual aspect of the downstairs bathroom is its wall covering of papier-mâché made from paper grocery bags. Dan created this wall covering using a "standard third-grade technique"of soaking the bags in Elmer's glue, squishing them onto the wall, and allowing them to dry. Some people might question the idea of covering bathroom walls with paper bags, but Dan says that the papier-mâché is no more vulnerable to water damage than wallpaper, which can be found on bathroom walls all over America. In the bathroom upstairs, Eric Farris used more tile designs to decorate the floor and tub area.

Papier-mâché walls in downstairs bath

Mosaic surrounding tub in upstairs bath

Even though Dan uses discarded and second-hand materials to construct his houses, he occasionally uses new materials as well. When he does choose to buy new appliances, he selects the best and most efficient he can find. He does not scrimp in costs on wiring or pipes, and he sometimes goes out of his way to ensure the energy efficiency of his houses.

One of the Charleston House's "green" features is a tankless water heater that warms the water for the kitchen and bathroom. As its name implies, this appliance heats water without storing it in a tank the way conventional water heaters do. Instead, it delivers heat to the water the instant the hot water tap is turned on. In order to accomplish this, the tankless water heater must use 54 amps, whereas a conventional water heater uses only 15. However, the tankless water heater still uses much less energy because instead of running constantly, it heats water only when hot water is needed.

Tankless water heater at top of stairs

Another "green" feature of the Charleston House is a 500-gallon cistern that sits in a shed-like structure behind the house, collecting rainwater for toilet flushing. Rainwater falls into a gutter that runs around the edge of the house and leads into the cistern. The gutter has a screen over it to prevent debris from falling into the water, but since the water is used only for toilet flushing, a few leaf particles cause no problems. The cistern can hold enough water for three months of toilet flushing, but Dan believes that it's possible to stretch it to six.

Dan described the insulation of the house in terms of R-value, a measure of thermal blockage. Higher R-values mean

Rainwater cistern

greater energy efficiency. Dan said that the house has an R-30 ceiling, R-19 walls, and an R-13 floor. He estimated the thickness of the walls to be six inches when you include the wall covering. He insulated the house with batt insulation made from fiberglass. Dan was also careful to prevent infiltration and built the house practically airtight, "like a Ziploc bag," to prevent leaks. In addition, he made sure to "go lean on the windows" for the sake of energy efficiency. Huge expanses of windows become thermal chimneys.

The Charleston House was designed by Dan and built by Phoenix Commotion, but it has also given other artists an opportunity to feature their work. Ray Blackard, one owner of the Charleston House, once noticed that the courtyard felt a little too secluded and thought that opening up its space would enable outsiders to see the house and appreciate its beauty. For this reason, The Phoenix Commotion held the Hole in the Wall competition, a contest for artists to submit designs for cutting holes in the wall of the courtyard. It was an art design competition open to anyone, and the grand prize winner would get to install it. Applicants from all over the country sent in designs for opening space in the walls, and a panel of judges finally selected Shannon Bryant to install her design on the front-side courtyard walls. The judges also chose Elizabeth Richardson's design for the right-side wall. Bryant,

Artistic installation inside the courtyard

Richardson, and the runners-up were awarded cash prizes for their designs. After cutting holes in the walls, the artists used colored glass bottles to fill the voids and add visual interest. Consequently, the towering walls appear less imposing while still offering the privacy that Dan envisioned.

Those who wish to live in the Charleston House should appreciate it as a structure built not just with cedar and yellow pine, but with soul and creative vision. The Phoenix Commotion even screens potential applicants to ensure that they recognize its uniqueness.

The first owners of the house, Alfredo Cerda and his wife, Susan Lowery, felt fortunate to live in it. Having rented a

Installation viewed from outside the courtyard

house for thirteen years, the couple dreamed of owning a home. Through a stroke of luck, Susan happened to notice a "For Sale" sign in front of the house as she drove past it. When she dialed the phone number written on the sign, she reached Dan. Before the completion of the deal, Dan handed Alfredo and Susan a key to the house and told them that they could spend a night there. The couple stayed for one night, ordered pizza, and decided to purchase the house. The transaction happened quickly, and Dan helped with the home-buying process. After that, Alfredo and Susan lived there for about seven years. They became friends with Dan, and he was always willing to come over and make repairs for the house when it needed them. He even taught Alfredo how to fix broken pipes in freezing weather.

After Alfredo took a job in the Houston area, he and Susan made the difficult decision to move out. Their next home was significantly larger, spanning 2,300 square feet, but they still missed the Charleston House. Alfredo described living there as exciting. The house served as a site for tours and even attracted news coverage from Houston's ABC 13 News and the *New York Times*. "Everyone who came over just adored our house," Alfredo recalled. Visitors often remarked on the scent of cedar. Alfredo and Susan had grown accustomed to it over time, but they noticed the scent again whenever they returned from a trip.

During their first two years of living there, the couple occasionally discovered some new detail of the house that they hadn't noticed before. They loved many of its features, such as the wood siding, decks, courtyard, and even the storage area under the stairs, which they dubbed "The Harry Potter Room." Susan didn't mind that the house lacked modern amenities, such as phone and cable jacks and a dishwasher. She appreciated the house's quirkiness, its history, and its compatibility with many possible decorating schemes because of its multi-colored floors.

Long after moving out, Susan still thought of the Charleston House as her house. Alfredo, likewise, spoke of the house with genuine affection and continued to carry his favorite pictures of it on his cell phone. It should not surprise anyone that the house profoundly affects those who have lived there. Alfredo and Susan were responding to a collaborative work of art, a creation of the members of Phoenix Commotion. When people develop strong connections to such a house, they reveal a characteristic of great art: its power to move people.

Rear view of the Charleston House

The Phoenix Commotion Gallery

The Victorian House

Victorian House turret

The Budweiser House

Budweiser box papier-mâché kitchen floor

The Ranch House

Ranch House bois d'arc staircase

The License Plate House

License Plate House bedroom ceiling

The Storybook House

Storybook House loft with closets underneath

Storybook House wine bottle exterior wall

The backyard shade of Storybook and Charleston Houses

The Charleston House

Charleston House broken-tile turtle mosaic floor

The Tree House

Tree House broken-china mosaic in Artist Studio

The Tree House Artist Studio

Frame Sample Ceiling inside the Tree House's Artist Studio

The Bone House

Bone House entrance gate from street

Bone patio furniture with Chevron Gazebo in background

The Bone House Artist Studio from Chevron Gazebo

Linda's House begins

Neko's Studio takes shape

Eric's House continues

The final touches on Eric's House

T.J. Burdett & Sons Recycling Center during construction

Uncle Sam mural from salvaged materials

Waste Management mural made from CDs, bottle caps, wine corks, etc.

Ongoing Community Artists' Wall at Smither Park

The Tree House

The Tree House: A Home in the Trees

by Donald R. Bates

A tree house evokes images of a childhood refuge built out of scrap lumber, complete with a sign on the entrance barring entry to female playmates. Yet long before the neighborhood kids scrambled up to their lofty clubhouse, humans were living in the relative safety and comfort of the trees. A habitat above the ground provided relief from the swarms of biting insects and hungry predators looking for a midnight snack.

Outside deck

When British explorer Captain James Cook claimed Tasmania for King George III in 1770, he found Aborigines living in the trees like "fauns and satyrs." Tasmanian tribesmen constructed thatched shelters in the tree canopy and lowered themselves to the ground in large baskets woven from coconut matting. In addition, some species of chimpanzees create simple nests in tree branches for sleeping. Perhaps the instinct to inhabit the trees is written deep inside the hominid genetic code.

A house that sits among the branches is also the perfect environment for an artist who seeks a closer relationship with nature—or the ability to look down on the motions of ground-based creatures in search of a fresh perspective. Perhaps Dan

Dan in a contemplative moment on walkway

Phillips considered all of these things when he set out to create an artist's residence unlike any other. More likely, Dan just thought it would be really cool to live in a tree. This unique structure can only be appreciated from inside the protective barrier that encircles it.

At first glance, the Tree House looks like something the Keebler elves might use for creating snack foods. The curved tree branches that create platforms and walkways resemble the fossilized rib cage of a gigantic prehistoric serpent. Poised thirty-five feet high in an enormous bois d'arc tree, the Tree House provides living and sleeping space for its occupants. On the ground below, Dan constructed a separate studio building that provides a convenient working space. The interior of the Hobbit-sized living area reveals a small but efficient room that is dominated by the trunk of the tree that supports the structure. Rising from the floor and extending through the ceiling, the tree, still very much alive, looks like a huge vertical column.

The rich wood veneer of the paneling that covers the walls, ceiling, and floors creates the impression of living inside an even larger hollow tree.

A skylight is mounted not on the ceiling, but rather into the floor, to allow occupants to peer down at the branches below. In the bedroom, Dan created a mosaic on the floor made out of discarded corks, donated by wine-loving friends. The spongy surface provided by the corks is delightful to walk on

The Tree House

with bare feet. Stained-glass panels emit splashes of red and pink light that shine down onto the floor like pools of spilled Merlot and Rosé. On the interior walls of his Tree House, Dan has mounted colorful plates and clear glass saucers that look as if an angry wood troll hurled them in all directions during a heated argument.

Invisible behind a nondescript façade in a quiet neighborhood near downtown Huntsville, the Tree House complex is easy to miss. Dan designed the entrance to the compound to match the funky style of the modest duplexes that surround it on 13th street. Next door, the Huntsville City Courthouse conducts daily business, oblivious to the artists who toil next door in the artist's studio. From the street, there is no hint of the fantasy world within. This has created a bit of a mythic reputation surrounding the home. Many local residents know of its existence but have no idea of the exact location.

"Surprisingly, a lot of people don't know this house is here," explains Dan. "Many residents will say that they have lived here for 30 years and didn't know there was a Tree House in Huntsville." Dan only leases the complex to artists, who must provide a portfolio of their work in order to be accepted as tenants.

The current occupant is graphic artist Charlie Oliver, his wife, and their four young children. Mr. Oliver is a tall young man with a neatly trimmed beard and eyes that gleam brightly when he discusses his passion for art. His neck and arms are adorned with colorful tattoos, and the polished silver gauges that he wears in both earlobes flash brilliantly in the Texas sun. In a soft voice with a fresh Michigan accent, Charlie explains how he discovered Dan's Tree House:

"This studio was available about the time our lease was

Charlie Oliver in the studio

coming up in Michigan—we were looking to try something new, so we packed up and came down to Huntsville."

Primarily working in digital media, Mr. Oliver has been able to expand into print making and large-format screen printing since moving into the Tree House complex.

Floor-mounted "skylight"

"This space has provided an opportunity to expand what we do," explains Charlie. "I've been teaching myself to do print making, which the studio space has been very helpful for. There is a sink and a place for me to clean all the stuff out of the tools. You need a space where if you spill a little ink you are not going to have to spend a ton of time having to clean. A lot of it is just to have a space to physically do the work."

The Tree House studio features extensive use of natural light with massive skylights in the ceiling that allow sunlight filtered by the surrounding trees to flow freely into the space below. "Natural light is huge in this studio, and that has really helped," Charlie says as he faces the large glass windows that reveal the outline of the house surrounded by a lattice of green and brown branches.

The Studio

Vintage gas heater in studio

> *When you are trying to draw a subject, to put together a creative idea, and trying to figure out: "If I align these two items together, where do the shadows fall?" The natural light is really helpful in those aspects. Also, when it comes to color, if you are mixing color, the light reflection off the red walls can contribute to a slightly different tone to your color. So having all the natural light in here really helps.*

The ceiling of the studio is composed of discarded picture frames of all shapes and colors, creating an angular mosaic. Dan also ensured that there are numerous electrical outlets for power tools, as well as multiple mirrors for dancers and performance artists. In the back, an industrial sink provides ample space for clean-up and a mixing station for pottery and ceramic work.

The appeal of living in a tree house can be infectious. Charlie and his wife host frequent artist's gatherings at the Tree House:

> *We encourage other people to do art. We have had art workshops, and this space has become not just our studio but a place where people in the community can come and learn new skills sets. We have had meals and music, and all kinds of different things have taken place in the studio that have allowed it to become a gathering place for all.*

Door mosaic made with frame samples, broken mirror, and 24k plates.

It's easy to picture the gathering of local art tribes, illuminated by the glowing fire pit beneath a starry sky, exchanging ideas while their children gleefully play on the platforms leading to the Tree House.

Of course, actually living in a tree does come with unique challenges. Without a foundation anchored to the ground, the Tree House is like a living creature and does not remain static like a normal house.

The Studio ceiling

"If you don't get seasick, it's a great place to live," says Charlie.

Now that we have been here for a couple of months, we don't notice it unless it's really windy. But the house is continually moving. When it's windy, you feel the tree move. Because of the branches, it sounds like something is going to come crashing through your house. The biggest thing for us was getting used to the movement of the house. At first, my wife said "I don't know if I can live here." One of the funny places that it is really noticeable is when you sit on the toilet, because it's attached to the floor of the house. When you are on the toilet, you move. Plus, you're not the only thing that lives in a tree. During the summer the click beetles get in—it's not unusual to find twenty or thirty beetles in the house and wake up with them crawling on you. I would compare living in the Tree House to camping. It's like camping out—only in a house.

The patio view

For anyone who has experienced the Swiss Family Robinson Tree House attraction at Walt Disney World Resort's Adventure Land, it is hard not to feel a sense of excitement when approaching the Tree House. Perhaps it's the primordial urge to live in the wel-

Bois d'arc branch walkway

coming arms of a sturdy tree that we share with our distant ancestors. Or maybe it's the chance to live like a child for a little while. Whatever the source, artists like Charlie Oliver are profoundly inspired by Dan's unusual residence: "I love it because our house is a very private sanctuary. I get up in the morning, I walk across the platform, and I can go right back to where I left off on my project the night before."

The Treehouse staircase

No doubt the artists who inhabit Dan Phillip's Tree House are influenced by the unique qualities of their leafy home. As they sleep in the snug arms of these protective boughs, the old spirits of the bois d'arc tree whisper secrets that seep into their dreams. Born the next day as splashes of green and brown in numerous works of art, these botanical reveries express the silent language of trees and invite the viewer to climb up from the mundane world on the ground and spend a few precious moments in the caring embrace of the trees.

Dan: Forever spreading the word

The Bone House

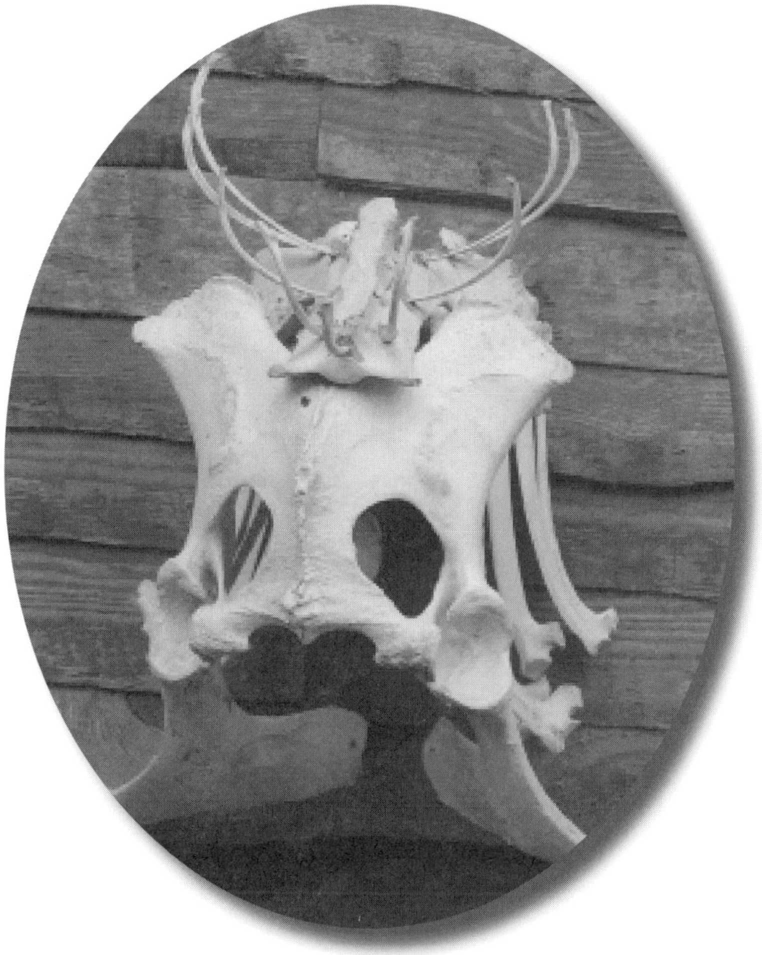

The Bone House

By Lauren McAuliffe

Tucked away on a shady, quiet street, behind wispy mimosas and towering magnolias, sits the Bone House. It is surrounded by dilapidated buildings and shrouded in trumpet vines. The first noticeable feature of the house is a wooden door, surrounded by foliage, featuring a glass pie dish for a window and a beef bone for a handle. The pie-dish window is opaque, etched glass, giving the door the appearance of a portal that hints at the creative whimsy that runs rampant on the other side. It is the only part of the house that is clearly visible from the street, but when it is opened, it reveals a wooden walkway that leads to the house itself.

Bone dog

Anyone strolling up the walkway is first greeted by the sculpture of a cheerful dachshund sitting on the banister. A close inspection reveals that the dog is actually constructed entirely of bones of different shapes and sizes. A mixture of the macabre and playful is a theme that is incorporated into every nook and cranny of the house.

Entering the Bone House, one experiences an immediate sense of wonder. Most homes reflect the personality of those who live in them in the color of the curtains, arrangement and style of the furniture, or themes of the artwork hanging on the walls. Without those little touches of individuality, most houses are simply buildings, little more than empty husks waiting to have life breathed into them by the fancies and knickknacks of those who will inhabit them. That impression is shattered upon walking into the Bone House. It exudes a personality all its own from the ceiling to the floor.

One of the first signs of that personality is the floor that stretches from the entryway into the kitchen. It is an undulating pattern made entirely of redwood, pine, and walnut shards, scraps of wood that would have been thrown away. Toward the back of the kitchen the wavy pattern comes together to

Kitchen area

form an image of a phoenix, with wings outstretched. The kitchen has a life of its own, with sections of beef bones inlaid into the countertop and fur-covered stools flanking one side of the counter. The stools, once discarded as trash, now add to the rustic aesthetic of the home.

To the left of the walkway is an open space that serves as one of the house's three bedrooms. Each bedroom comes with a bathroom, and the one downstairs is truly unique. The walls, ceiling, and floor of the bathroom are completely covered in broken pieces of mirror. The bathroom stands as a testimony to Dan's motto that repetition creates pattern. Shards of broken glass would be discarded by most people as useless, but give Dan a pile of them and he will give you a bathroom that lends a whole new meaning to the idea of a fortress of solitude and opens up a relatively small space by using reflective light.

Repetition is used throughout the house to create not only patterns and consistency, but also variety. One of the bedrooms upstairs, for example, has a floor that is made entirely of wine corks. Dan calls it the Dr. Scholl's floor because all of the cork creates a springy effect when it is walked on.

Wine-cork floor

Not only is the cork floor comfortable to walk on: It is also stylistically impressive, as the corks are arranged in eye-catching circular patterns. Another place where pattern comes into play is in one of the bedrooms, where the floor is made of bottle caps from all different brands of beverages. It is similar to the cork floor because it utilizes donated materials and repetition but unique in that the caps add a variety of colors to the room. Another of the bathrooms has a floor that is covered in beer labels. The labels are laid over one another for a patchwork effect and then soaked in a clear laminate. Using this technique, the possibilities for floor coverings are nearly limitless.

Every space in the bone house has its own personal touch that makes it stand out from every other space. For example, although many places in the home use bone for either decoration or function, each place is clearly created with thought and care.

Stairs with bone trim

The staircase has sections of thick beef bone that are inlaid into each stair and smaller more delicate bones that decorate the railings. Bone is used throughout the house, giving it its name. As Dan says, "The only difference between bone and ivory is that ivory is expensive and illegal and bone is legal and

Bone Patio Furniture

free." Dan acquired the bone he used throughout the Bone House from ranchers' bone yards. He explained that he puts the word out for materials like bone and wine corks, and people of the community are always there to supply him with all he needs and more.

Not only is bone abundant in the design—it is also used creatively to emphasize certain aspects of the house. On the heavy double doors that separate the back patio from the front yard, thick femur bones are used. On something more subtle, such as the banister of the stairway, thinner and more delicate bones are used to create a complementary effect. The courtyard walls are decorated with pelvic bones because they have an intricate pattern, almost like that of a conch shell that has been halved.

Recyled flowers by crew

The courtyard has an entire set of patio furniture, all constructed of bone, of course. There are also piles of bone arranged around the grill and garden for the artists of the home to use however they wish. These piles include cow skulls, various beef bones, armadillo shells, and turtle shells. There is even a chandelier accented with small bones that hangs in the artists' studio. With so much bone throughout the home, it might seem that the atmosphere could become rather morbid. On the contrary, all of the materials are arranged and incorporated in such a way that they create more of a sense of lightheartedness.

Outdoor grilling area

Part of the reason that the house, along with all of Dan's other houses, has so much personality is that Dan's real focus in

Bone House resident Bob Maninger is an avid hunter.

his project is the people who are involved. The Bone House was built specifically for artists. Dan is very adamant about supporting the artists of a community because they enrich it.

The house comes complete with a greenhouse that is constructed, among other things, with glass doors that were donated by the owner of the Café Texan. It also has an outdoor grilling area with walls made of different colored wine bottles and an awning that is made from two discarded Chevron signs.

In addition to all of these luxuries, the Bone House was built with a studio out back. The walls of the studio are lined completely with CDs in a pattern that mimics the scales of a fish. On the back wall there is a large window, which lets in ample amounts of light for any type of artwork. Dan explained

Front Room

Crew member Josh Starkey shapes mirror shards.

that the studio was designed to accommodate artists working in every medium. There is large open space and a wall of mirrors for dancers. There is also plenty of light for painters and numerous electrical outlets for tools such as a pottery wheel and kiln. Dan only asks that whichever artist that applies to live in one of his houses, whether he is a sculptor or a musician, have a portfolio that he is working on building. The dedication to providing opportunities to groups of people who have too often been discarded by society is inherent in every aspect of the Bone House.

Dan's humanitarian spirit is infections, not only for those who live in his homes, but for those who work to build them. One of his workers who helped build the Bone House moved across the country simply because he heard about The Phoenix Commotion from a friend and was interested in joining the effort. He had already attained a degree in metal-smithing and jewelry making but was so intrigued with the program that he immediately moved to Hunsville to try and be a part of it. In the six months that he has been on the job he has learned how to frame and build a house as well as complete many independent projects, such as tiling a bathroom with shards of mirror. He also has dreams of starting his own building project, which will allow him to refurbish old buildings in Nashville using many of Dan's techniques. He says of Dan, "It's remarkable how genuine and trusting he is. He tends to attract quality individuals."

The Bone House stands as a testament to the types of people Dan attracts: those who are willing to work hard and learn to find possibility in piles of junk. It is clear that Dan not only sees the potential in discarded materials—he also sees the potential in every person he comes in contact with. The Bone House is just one example of how he builds on that potential until it is reached.

Achieving the goals that Dan and his crew set for themselves is not always easy, and the Bone House demonstrates just how determined the people involved in The Phoenix Commotion are. In 2009 the original Bone House burned down due to causes which have not been determined. The only part of the house that was not destroyed in the fire was the walkway and door.

Facing such a loss was difficult as the crew had to completely start over, but the community was there to support them. Many people, including some of Dan's old students, left supportive letters on the door to offer their condolences and prayers. One note read, "We rise from the ashes." The Bone House, as it stands today, is a perfect representation of the phoenix, which symbolizes Dan's efforts. It literally burned to the ground, but because of the dedication of those who would not accept defeat, it rose from the ashes to be reborn. It is a testament to hard work and creativity. It represents a spirit which will not be kept down, which will always rise from the ashes.

The Homestead Initiative

The Homestead Initiative: A New American Dream

by Doug Haines

How far that little candle throws his beams! So shines a good deed in a weary world. ~William Shakespeare

There are two basic threads that make up Dan Phillips' Phoenix Commotion. The first would be the ground-up projects that he and his minimum-wage crew build together from start to finish to sell to clients. This is the business side. The other side of The Phoenix Commotion is the humanitarian side: a mentor program that Dan often refers to as the Homestead Initiative. This program stems out of Dan's core belief that housing should be a birthright and not just a privilege. As Dan says, "You gotta live somewhere." By providing those with lower incomes with the skills, the know-how, and the encouragement needed to build their own homes, he is providing them the opportunity to weigh in on the basic human need for shelter, and he's helping them do it on their own terms.

Dan Phillips and The Phoenix Commotion are

Josh Starkey works on his roof.

Crew member Josh Starkey's house

considered by many around the world to be both innovators and a driving force in the current micro-housing movement. After learning his lesson with the Budweiser House, Dan has been downsizing ever since. One of the philosophies behind The Phoenix Commotion is that people need to learn to guard against the market-based economy mentality. "Of course, the realtor wants to steer you towards buying the bigger house—more house equals more commission," explains Phillips. "Building a house yourself, though, is a big undertaking. And when it's finished, you're whipped—that's why we build'm so small."

The Homesteader houses, like all of Dan's projects, push the ideas of sustainability, recycling, and repurposing. Dan explains that 75-85% of the materials used in these houses are recycled and/or repurposed. He never buys new, unless he has to. "Some things you just have to buy new, like wire, plumbing, fans, insulation, roofing, paint, and adhesives. But the intrinsic value of the house, the structure itself, is usually made up of about 95% recycled or repurposed materials."

When building a home, the majority of the cost is in the labor. Even Dan's minimum-wage crew tends to consume about 85% of his budget. This puts the final cost of a normal Phoenix Commotion house, even as thrifty as they are, out of many people's reach. By removing the labor cost and showing the aspiring homeowners how to build and maintain the house themselves, Dan greatly reduces the cost and makes the seemingly impossible dream of owning a home a reality. As a mentor, Dan makes only $10 per square foot, and since the houses are so small, this ends up being a minimal expense for the homeowner/builder, especially considering what Dan brings to the table. "Heck, that wouldn't even pay for my funeral," he jokes.

George Boone starts his foundation.

These houses generally begin at 240 square feet, the minimum square footage allowed by the state. He then adds on 100 square feet per occupant. This means that a house built for a couple with no children would need to be a mere 340 square feet. To most of us, this seems ridiculously small, but Dan is a firm believer in doing more with less, and it is all part of his ongoing effort to downsize the American Dream and make us all realize that we have become slaves to our possessions. Of course, Dan also understands that a family's needs may change over time. This is why he also includes an insulated porch with ceiling, complete with electrical outlets, equal to half the allowed square footage of the house itself in the plans that he gives to the prospective owner/builder. This means that a couple building a 340-square-foot house can have a 170-square-foot porch that can easily be walled in, thus making it an easy addition to the home, which will create more room for the growing family. And since by this point the builder will have already built the original home, he will possess all the skills needed to complete the addition himself. "If you want a bigger house, then just add on to the one you've got," Dan explains. This is the beauty of The Phoenix Commotion's Homesteader Initiative: It is all about empowerment and giving people the tools to do it themselves.

Shannon Bryant helps on George's Foundation.

Framing begins on George's house.

After discovering Dan and The Phoenix Commotion on the internet, Neko Richardson became "infected with the idea." She immediately got in touch with Dan through The Phoenix Commotion website and was amazed at how quickly and "organically" things began to happen.

As a mentor, Dan demonstrates and explains each step of the process to the aspiring builders, so that they can take it from there. Of course, there are some more technical aspects that Dan handles himself, like electrical work and plumbing, but the homeowners/builders are still a part this process, assisting him as he runs wires or installs pipes.

Many of Dan's homesteaders, like Neko, work with Dan on his crew during the week and work on their own homes on the weekends. As Neko explains, "Anyone can do this, but I highly recommend joining the crew. It's like getting free lessons during the week that you can take home and use on your own place. I constantly find myself applying the tricks I learned during the week." She then goes on to explain the importance of getting to know the man behind the idea. "If you want to build a home like Dan, you have to get to know Dan. You have to build a relationship with him. He inspires you and shows you that there's another way to live. We have other choices—a new American Dream. It's life changing."

Besides teaching and demonstrating how to actually build the house, Dan also acts as a liaison with things like jurisdiction and inspectors, which can often feel overwhelming to first-time homeowners/builders. They still have to pull all the permits themselves, but Dan is there to help them with the process and point them in the right direction when things get complicated or confusing. He also provides advice about financing, scheduling, and insurance. For example, Dan recommends insurance companies that offer homeowner's insurance with a builder's-risk rider during the construction. This policy protects the homeowner/builder in the case of unforeseen things like fire, but it also provides liability coverage as well.

The main requirement to become a part of Dan's Homesteader Initiative, besides a commitment to the micro-housing movement, is that the potential homeowner/builder not have bad credit. Good or no credit at all is fine. This is because Dan has found that the banks are very supportive of this project "as long as it's a reasonable risk. If they have to foreclose, everybody loses." The draw schedule for the interim loan begins

with the property, and then the foundation, and so on. After the building of the house is completed, the loan rolls into a permanent financing home loan—a mortgage.

By the time the homesteader finishes the house, the mortgage is usually only around $300 a month, including taxes and insurance. It's a startlingly low number, plus they own their own house and will take care of it, thus building equity. And they'll know how to take care of it because they built it. They'll know every nook and cranny. They'll even know its problem areas, or as Dan calls them, "demons," before they ever move in. Calling a repairman will become a thing of the past. As Neko puts it, "It's economic liberation.

"We'll no longer be dependent on others for daily household repairs. Building and repairing homes is language we all used to be fluent in 70 years ago, but we've forgotten. Dan is reminding us of where we came from, and he brings us back to our roots."

Perhaps the most important thing that Dan Phillips brings to the table as a mentor is his unique philosophy and his ability to encourage and inspire others not only to think outside the box, but to believe whole-heartedly in themselves and their abilities. Often after the foundation and the initial structure have been erected, both the project and the builders tend to experience what Dan calls "a midterm lag." It looks like a house, but there is still a lot left to be done, and the progress that is being made is not something that is easily recognizable to the eye. Small details and things like electrical work and plumbing, for example, are vital to the home's completion—they have to be done, but they are not things that can be seen from the street as progress. It begins to look like nothing is moving forward, like things are at a complete standstill without any advancement. This becomes very hard on the home-

owners'/builders' state of mind. They become discouraged. They begin to feel embarrassed, perhaps even like failures. Work begins to slow down. This is not only hard on them, but it is also hard on the City. Besides the eyesore of an incomplete house, there is also the matter of all the files and permits that have to be left open during the construction process. "Those folks for the city work really hard and they're severely underfunded," Phillips explains. At this point, when encouragement is no longer enough, Dan and his crew come to the rescue and help to jumpstart the project and get it back on track. For this reason, pretty much all of Dan's homesteaders will agree that Dan Phillips is the best ten dollars they've ever spent, as he helps them press through the difficult times.

"Yes, it's hard, but so is a 30-year mortgage," Neko says. "And when I'm done, I'm done. It's paid for. It's my retirement." Richardson has a budget of only $16,000 for her home and studio that she is building. She describes herself as a "workaholic," hard at work to change her life in a "positive way."

Dan gives glass-cutting lesson to a volunteer.

Currently, she is in the process of finishing up her 350-square-foot studio, and she will live in the studio until the house is completed. Finding other houses she sees to be "annoyingly normal," Richardson takes great pride in her work and loves the fact that her home and studio will speak of "soul and depth and diversity" when all is said and done. One of her favorite aspects of her new home is the porch, which she has painted all kinds of different colors. "There's no other porch like it," she says with a smile. This obvious pride in Neko Richardson comes not only from a place of ownership, but from a sense of craftsmanship—from a job well done. And without the burden of a $1,200-a-month mortgage, she understands that her "choices in life are now much broader," thanks to Dan Phillips.

The City of Huntsville is unique and very supportive of Dan and his green-micro-housing movement. He feels fortunate to live in a place that understands his vision. The Homestead Initiative, like any other Dan Phillips project, is about changing the world for the better. It is about showing people what can be done, if they can just break free from the market-based mindset that has plagued this country in recent years. It is about sustainability. It is about hard work and about giving people the skills and the opportunity to change their lives in a positive way.

Josh Starkey on finished roof

T. J. Burdett and Sons Recycling Center

T. J. Burdett and Sons Recycling Center

By Christina Fernandez

Waste not the smallest thing created, for grains of sand make mountains, and atomies infinity. ~Eric Knight

Considering the crew's dedication to recycling and repurposing materials for all of their projects, it comes as no surprise that the first commercial building to be erected by Dan Phillips and The Phoenix Commotion would be a recycling center. When T.J. Burdett first founded his company, he ran it from his house on Avenue M in Huntsville, Texas. As the business began to grow, the recycling center was moved to its current location off of I-45, and Burdett eventually passed the business down to his sons.

The new T.J. Burdett and Sons Recycling Center office building is as unique

in its construction as it is hard to miss. A giant Uncle Sam on the backside of the building facing the interstate is built completely from salvaged materials and points at passing cars exclaiming, "I want your can!" The tip of his finger is an old sink strainer and his curly hair is made from aluminum shavings. To Sam's immediate right, one finds the title of the company spelled out in other repurposed materials, such as the retired motorcycle fender that has been used to make the "R" and the "Y" made from a discarded engine compartment. The "C" is contained within the circular green-arrowed recycling symbol, which spins freely in the wind.

The next thing that one notices is that the building appears to be built slightly askew. This is, Dan explains, "an optical illusion." Dan and the crew purposely slanted the roof to give the building a "dynamic" look. In actuality, the walls of the structure are like any other; the only difference is that curved pieces of wood have been added to the studs to give the impression that the building is bowed.

When looking at the building from the front, the doorway also appears to be dramatically tilted to one side. Again, this is an illusion. "Only the doorjamb and casing are curved. The door itself is actually perfectly rectangular," Dan explains. This was done by kerfing the wood. Kerfing is a term used to indicate that a tool has been used to produce a notch or cut in the wood. In this case, Dan used a circular saw to make the notches. After making several ¼ inch deep notches in the wood, each spaced about an inch apart, the wood becomes easier to manipulate and can be bent into whatever angle is desired. In order to keep the chosen shape in place, spacers are then used to hold the wood in that position, while the frame is nailed against the structure. Using his wood-working skills, Dan then decorated the doorframe with a beautiful vine-like design carved into a 2X6 piece of redwood, which helps to conceal the kerfs from view.

Upon entering the offices of T.J. Burdett and Sons, one is struck by the fact that many of the walls are built from stacked non-linear slabs of granite, giving the interior a rustic and unconventional look.

Texas star mosaic

These slabs are held together by Liquid Nails to keep them in place, and their colors lack conformity, varying from whites to greys to pinkish tones. The floor is also made from discarded granite, and in the middle of the room there is a mosaic of the Texas star. Each piece of granite that was chosen for this floor is unique in its own right. Dan, through the years, has become a big fan of creating mosaics out of granite. "You get to relish all the permutations of granite."

Stacked granite and radiator walls

The ceiling has been plastered with CDs, which brighten the room when illuminated by the efficient fluorescent bulbs. There is an upstairs area that will be used for storage, and the walls and bannister leading up to the second floor are decorated with pieces from old metal road signs cut into different shapes. The reds, yellows, oranges, whites, and blues from the signs seem to glow beneath the fluorescents, as words like *workers*, *welcome*, *slow*, and *Texas* pop out from every direction.

As for the office spaces, the first one will be occupied by the supervisor so that he can keep an eye on the yard. The doorknob to this office is made from a ball-peen braised onto a steel rod. Directly across from the doorway, one notices a rainbow of colors reflecting in the light. This effect was created by embedding pieces of stained glass within the granite wall. In the second office, the walls are built from the repurposed radiators salvaged from old cars and trucks, which are very effective at reducing outside noise. The doorknob is a hood ornament from a car. The third office also has a hood ornament for a doorknob, but its walls are built out of corrugated sheets. Each office has its own window A/C unit with a heat pump. Dan uses these heat pumps because they are ductless and energy efficient.

Hood-ornament doorknob

Kitchen countertop

The bathroom in the office building features a vintage-looking vanity sink and marble-tiled shower and flooring. After installing the sink, Dan learned from one of his Swedish exchange students, who was raised on a farm, that the actual name of the sink translates to mean "cow cup." In its former life, this sink had most likely been used as a trough. The kitchen, located next to the bathroom, has a counter made out of granite. The strip of wall above it also contains marble. The dark colors of this section of the room create a dramatic contrast to the lighter ones found on the walls and floors.

Road signs and granite

The T. J. Burdett office building is a one-of-a-kind creation. With its recycled Uncle Sam mural and bowed-looking exterior, it catches the attention of anyone who passes it on the interstate. The interior of the building is equally unique with its granite-stacked walls, repurposed road signs and car radiators, and reflective CD ceiling. Drenched in the spirit of both the Phoenix Commotion and the recycling center which it houses, the building seems to embrace the beauty and adaptability of salvaged materials.

View from I-45

WM
WASTE MANAGEMENT

Waste Management

Public Arts Project

Waste Management Education Center

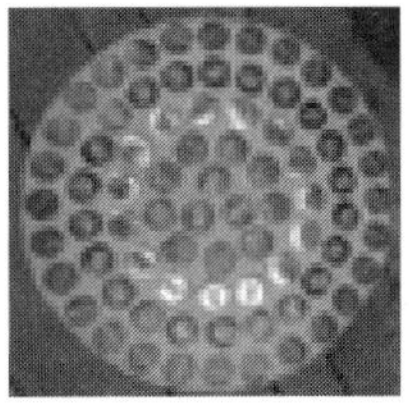

by Amanda Dellett

It is not every day that The Phoenix Commotion gets, or even wants, the opportunity to work with a large corporation. After all, large corporations typically hire a design committee, and those committees are often forced to come up with design ideas that conform to the many standards set by the hiring corporation, which means that the usual result is somthing beige.

However, when Waste Management contacted Dan Phillips about designing an education center located at their Gasmer recycling facility in Houston, it was a creativity challenge that he readily accepted. Waste Management's mission is similar to The Phoenix Commotion's: Both believe in the concept of sustainability, reducing society's use of the Earth's natural resources and reusing or recycling items that we already have in order to reduce our carbon footprint. Waste Management processes 9,000 tons of commercial and residential recycling materials each month. Their goal with the education center was to create a room where children and adults can come to see creative recycling all around them.

Another reason Dan decided to get involved with the project is that Waste Management was willing to give him free reign over the entire 800-square-foot space. They had seen the previous projects completed by Dan and The Phoenix Commotion and knew that his design ideas would be right in line with their mission. The team, which consisted of nine artists and builders, began the project in the summer of 2010. They

Matt Gifford in a moment of narcissism

worked together designing the large murals in the artists' studio of the Bone House and then transported them to Waste Management for installation. The only purchased materials used in the design of the room were the glue and fasteners—everything else was rescued from a landfill and repurposed.

The finished room is a treat for the eyes. The first thing you notice is the dozens of unique chairs set in the middle of the space, one created out of used tires, another out of cabinet doors. Many have been painted vibrant colors or "bejeweled" with bottle caps. The seat of one chair is composed of tightly woven plastic grocery bags. This is where classrooms full of children will sit when they visit the center to learn about the benefits of recycling. Under their feet, they will see a beautiful papier-mâché floor created out of recycled paper grocery sacks. Above their heads is a glistening ceiling.

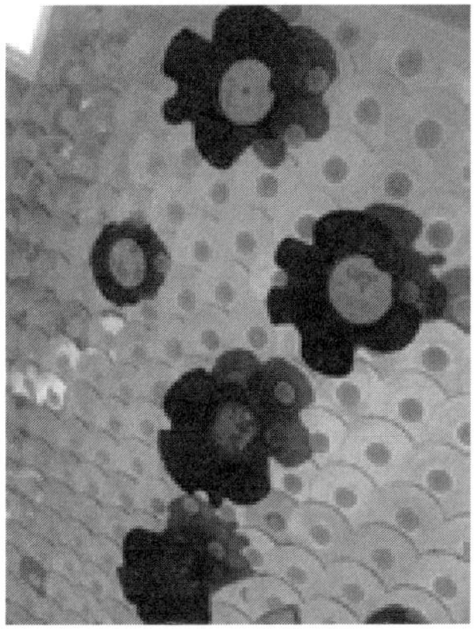

However, the real eyecatcher in the room is the large, expansive mural that surrounds you on every side. This mural tells an important story for anyone who visits the center. It starts with a Waste Management truck dumping its contents into the landscape. These contents eventually take form as books, a car, and even a rendition of the Storybook House, a real project that The Phoenix Commotion completed in Huntsville back in 2008. The next wall depicts a majestic forest, which on the last wall develops into a wondrous tropical scene of palm trees. The idea is to show how common items can be recycled or repurposed and how the environment will benefit. The forests are lush and vibrant, and the tropical scene is light and airy, a testament to the benefits of clean air.

The wall mosaics are created out of a variety of repurposed items, from broken ceramic tile to old dishes. The playful mixture of colors as well as texture beckons you forward for closer inspection. If you look closely at the contents spilling out of the truck, you will spot an array of everyday things that we take for granted, such as a mug, an old cabinet door, or the lid to a pot. There are even items that the average person would immediately throw away, like the lids to cleaning products or empty cat food cans—things that all of us consider "junk" but that are composed of recyclable materials that too often find their way to landfills.

The forest was constructed of papier-mâché by using old magazines. The artists created depth by laying magazines in a vertical pattern in the background and designing bigger, more detailed trees in the foreground. There is also a path that leads your eyes deep into the forest. The trees are in beautiful shades of blues, purples, and grays, yet upon closer inspection you can actually read the text from the pages of the magazines used to create the trunks and sprawling branches.

The forest floor is "littered" with small ferns, flowers, and even animals created out of "trash." The forest eventually becomes sparse, with the last tree appearing to release dozens of butterflies into a light and airy space. The mural then takes on a more damask pattern, created from more grocery sacks.

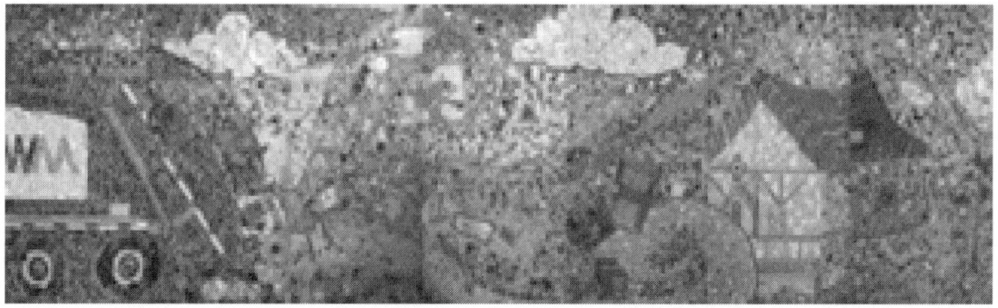

Children visiting the center to learn about recycling will be unable to deny the beauty that can be found in everyday things. The work of art that encompasses them from floor to ceiling will no doubt serve as a source of inspiration, which will then hopefully pass on to future generations. The Phoenix Commotion's work with Waste Management is not only a huge step for passing along the message of sustainability, but a sign that the movement is growing to reach even larger audiences.

Smither Park
In memory of John H. Smither (1940-2002)

The Smither Park Project

The Smither Park Project: Creating Art & Community

by Doug Haines

"A work of art is the unique result of a unique temperament.
~Oscar Wilde

Postman Jeff McKissack created only one piece of art in his entire life, The Orange Show monument, and it took him 25 years. He was not driven or influenced by contemporary art or pop trends. His vision came from somewhere inside. As Stephanie Smither explains, "He felt it in his heart and soul."

Volunteers work on Memory Wall.

In 1980, inspired by McKissack's creation, Marilyn Oshman founded The Orange Show Center for Visionary Art in the southeast end of Houston, Texas. The foundation owns and operates The Beer Can House, a well-known Houston landmark, and produces the annual Houston Art Car Parade. Its most recent venture is Smither Park, located on the 1/2-acre lot adjacent to The Orange Show in the east end of town at 2402 Munger Street. The park is an elaborate collaboration among

Jeff McKissack

the Smither family, The Orange Show Center for Visionary Art, and the community that hosts it. It will feature the always sustainable artistic vision of Dan Phillips, who will oversee and render the architectural structures drafted by Eubanks Architects and installed by Goodchild Builders.

The Smither family has been involved with the The Orange Show and their projects since 1988, and the park will be a monument to the memory of Stephanie Smither's late husband, John H. Smither, who passed away in 2002. It is also meant to be a gift to both the eastside neighborhood where it resides and to the city itself. As Phillips puts it, "Everybody loves a park, but this park is special." Built by the community under Dan's direction, Smither Park will forever be a testament to the vibrancy and creativity of the city of Houston and its citizens by being the city's first folk-art inspired green space, while still maintaining the philosophy and aesthetics of the world-renowned Orange Show monument.

John Smither's widow, Stephanie

The creation and the existence of Smither Park speaks to a sense of community—a community with an artistic side raring to get out and be explored through the textures and shapes of folk art. The park itself is designed to be a sculpture, but unlike most sculptures, Smither Park requires a high level of interaction from all who view it. It beckons to the artist in

Dan at work in Park

all of us and provides a much needed outlet for the creativity that is all too often suppressed by the hustle and bustle of the modern world.

Artist Kate Kendall works on her sculpture.

Because of this suppression, Dan offers art workshops for anyone who feels the urge to jump in and get their creative feet wet by getting involved with the project. In these community workshops, Dan shares tricks of the trade and helps those in attendance find both their artistic vision and voice so that they can help build and embellish the park as it grows. For example, he shows them how to make figures pop out from the wall by using chicken wire and filling it in with Styrofoam (or other light-weight fillers) and then covering it with mortar. This creates a three-dimensional effect and gives the wall even more texture and personality. It is all about textures, shapes, and images of people being people.

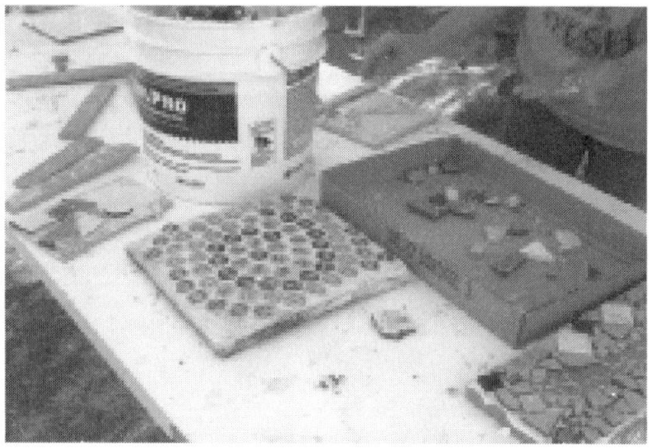

Smither Park is about two main things: the human experience and, like all Dan Phillips' projects, sustainability. "We're all about recycling and repurposing," Phillips explains. He goes on to

discuss the importance of picking the right materials for the job. "They have to be materials that will last. Houston has some pretty severe weather." Dan and the park's commitment to sustainability and recycling inspires the decorative elements

Dan gives glass-cutting tutorial.

throughout the park by exploring the reuse and repurposing of materials like broken china, bottle caps, bone, tile shards, and sea shells, which will be fashioned into the various designs

that bring Smither Park to life. Phillips describes the outcome as "eye-candy" or "a smörgåsbord for the eye."

Smither Park will provide its community with many amazing and inviting attractions that are meant to be enjoyed by anyone and everyone. On the east end of the park, visitors will find The Amphitheatre, a.k.a. The Grotto, with its colorful mosaics and an interior of uniquely patterned mirror-shard designs. This exciting atmosphere will be able to host any number of various staged performances for people to enjoy. It will also be the perfect place for other events, like weddings, quinceañeras, and family reunions.

Another attraction will be the Meditation Garden in the park. This area will give people an escape from the fast pace of everyday life while they relax and listen to the soothing trickle of the water wall, which runs on recycled rain water. The park will also host the 400 ft. Memory Wall, which will provide a place for friends and families to honor and remember their loved ones. Just beyond the Memory Wall, The Serpentine Tunnel and half tunnel will create a number of interesting areas for activities with spaces for tables and benches to accommodate small group gatherings.

The Squire family gets involved.

Volunteers work on Memory Wall.

There will also be the 12 ft. Tower, which will house a custom-built "coin roll." Here visitors can watch their quarters follow any number of pathways through a mesmerizing maze.

And what would a park be without something purely for the children, or least the child in all of us? Near a small grove of orange trees will be the Long-Sweep Swing inviting children of all ages to delight in the simple pleasure of swinging and having fun. Throughout the park, open spaces and walkways will be decorated with hopscotch and mosaics, guaranteeing everyone who visits Smither Park an opportunity for family fun and activities accessible to all. It truly is a special place to be.

Kate Kendall adjusts her design.

At Smither Park, everyone is encouraged to get involved. Anyone interested in donating to the project or participating in one of Dan's art workshops can find out more by visiting www.orangeshow.org.

Gena Atwell (left) and Stephanie Smither work on their collaborative sculpture of a mermaid.

Artist Matt Gifford tweaks his sculpture.

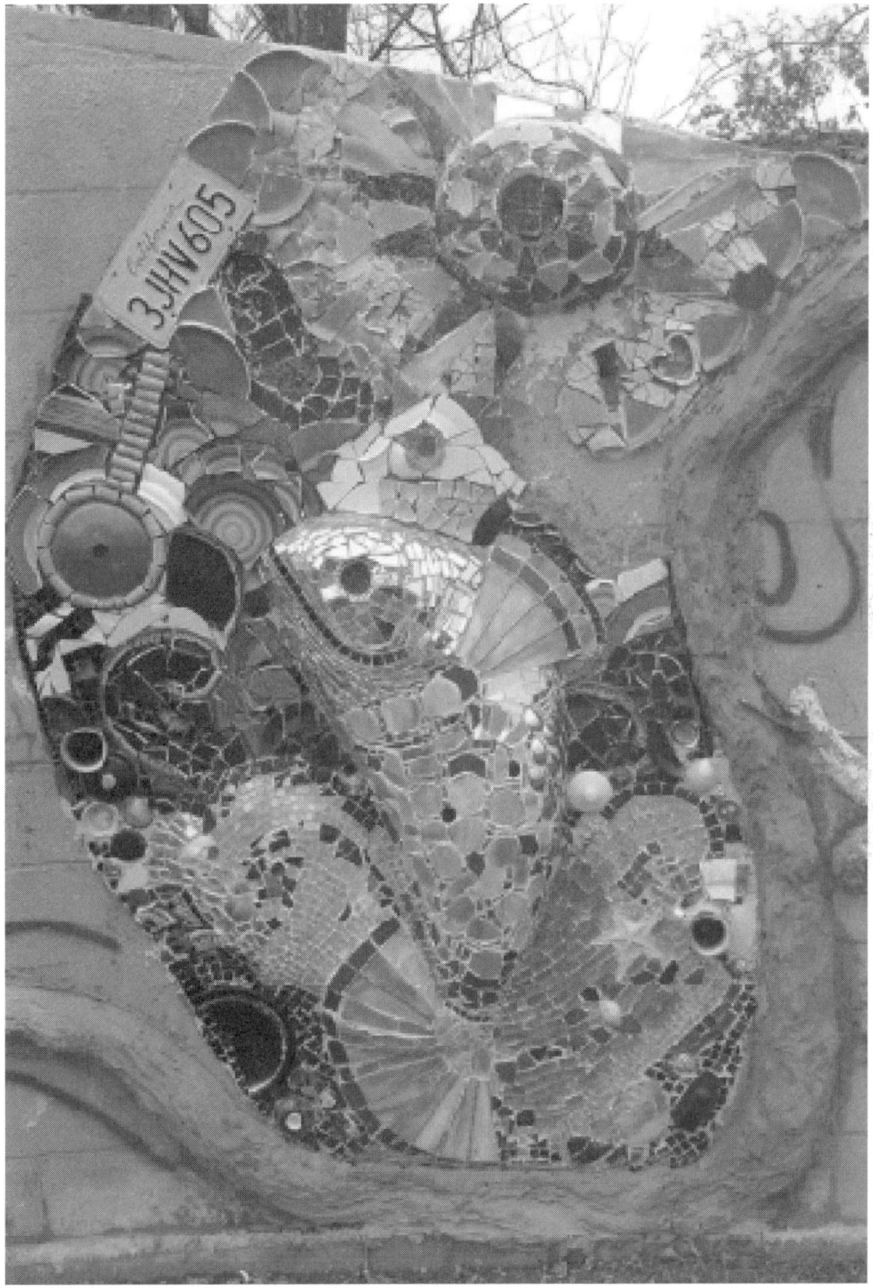

The Editors

Amanda Dellett is a graduate student at SHSU.

Don R. Bates is an English Instructor at Lone Star College in Houston, Texas. He earned his MA in creative writing at Sam Houston State University in 2012. Don is currently editing his first novel, *Vanitas*.

Christina Fernandez has a Masters in English. She is currently working on finishing a novel and resides in Spring, Texas.

Jake Gebhardt is a graduate student at SHSU.

Doug Haines worked for Texas Review Press for two years while pursuing his MA in English at Sam Houston State University. A professional musician and songwriter, he is currently completing his MFA in Fiction at the University of Memphis and teaching freshman composition.

Anna Jennings is an adjunct instructor of English at Sam Houston State University. She plans to spend years honing her teaching skills. She reads about twenty webcomics, shops at thrift stores, and drinks coffee compulsively.

Dustin Levien graduated from Sam Houston State University with a Bachelor of Arts in English in 2009 and completed a Master of Arts in English at SHSU in 2011. He is currently teaching English as a Second Language at an elementary school in Nonsan, South Korea.

Lauren McAuliffe is a graduate student at SHSU.

Margaret Miller Sellers is a graduate student at SHSU.